Mission-Driven Money

Mission-Driven Money

How Purpose Fuels Profit
(A Bold Guide to Wealth with Impact)

Nico Farouq

Mindful Pages

Published in 2025

ISBN: 9789371341080 (PB)
ISBN: 9789371345019 (eBook)

Published by

Mindful Pages
Imprint of Alpha Editions LLC
312 W. 2nd St #1834
Casper, WY 82601, USA

Content

Introduction
Why the World Needs Mission-Driven Money Now

There's more wealth in the world today than at any other point in history. Capital flows freely, markets are swelling, and technological progress has made opportunity more accessible than ever. But look a little closer—beneath the surface of affluence and advancement, something fundamental seems to have slipped through the cracks. Quietly, and often uncomfortably, many of today's top achievers—executives, founders, and rising stars alike—confess to feeling a strange emptiness. They've climbed the ladder, reached the milestones, filled their calendars with success—and yet, what they've arrived at feels curiously hollow. This isn't a flaw in character or ambition; it's a sign of a broader misalignment. Somewhere along the way, we mistook money for meaning.

This book begins by calling that condition what it is: the great disconnect. It's the unsettling gap between material success and a deeper sense of fulfilment. Of course, money still matters—it grants agency, provides comfort, and opens doors. But it no longer holds the cultural weight it once did as the singular gauge of a life well lived. The traditional signposts of achievement—titles, income, reach—are proving to be poor proxies for genuine satisfaction. People are waking up to the hard truth: profit without purpose doesn't fill the soul. More often than not, it leaves them exhausted, disengaged, and questioning what it was all for.

What makes this era especially significant isn't just that the old definitions are faltering, but that something new and credible is taking their place. We are witnessing a quiet but powerful shift—the rise of what thinkers and economists are increasingly referring to as the purpose economy. In this new landscape, meaning isn't just nice to have—it's becoming a serious strategic asset. Consumers are spending with their values in mind. Employees, particularly the younger cohort, want more than a paycheque—they want purpose. Even investors, once single-minded in their pursuit of returns, are looking at impact as part of the equation. The evidence is difficult to ignore: organisations that bake purpose into their DNA tend to perform better—not just ethically, but economically too.

This isn't theory. It's happening. Brands anchored in mission are outpacing their peers across sectors—be it fashion, fintech, food, or beyond. Social enterprises, once relegated to the margins, are now shaping mainstream models. The most coveted workplaces today? They're the ones offering more than just perks—they offer a chance to contribute to something that matters. Purpose has moved out of the realm of philanthropic garnish and into the heart of competitive advantage.

Still, despite the growing momentum, many remain stuck in an outdated script. Nowhere is this more visible than in the cult of hustle. Somewhere along the line, we conflated busyness with value and began mistaking burnout for dedication. We inherited a work culture that idolises exhaustion and treats rest as an indulgence instead of a necessity. But truly—what is the point of wealth if we sacrifice our health, integrity, or relationships to get it? Today's professional stands at a crossroads: driven to succeed, but increasingly unwilling to pay with their peace of mind. What's needed isn't a new app for time management—it's a rethink of what it even means to be productive. Not just output, but impact. Not just activity, but legacy.

This book proposes a bold reframe: that business can, and should, be a force for meaningful change. It takes aim at the tired dichotomy that insists one must choose between doing good and doing well. That notion—that purpose is somehow at odds with profit—isn't just misleading; it's been repeatedly disproven. In reality, purpose-driven organisations often show greater resilience, attract better talent, and earn stronger trust from the public. The idea that ethics erode competitiveness simply doesn't hold up under scrutiny.

But don't be mistaken—this isn't just another book about branding or CSR. It's a manifesto for a new breed of entrepreneur. One who sees money not as a destination, but as a means. One who's done with transactional success and hungry for something transformational. Whether you're a seasoned leader craving a deeper sense of direction, a founder balancing passion with profit, or an aspiring changemaker still sketching your vision—this book is written with you in mind. You're not a bystander in this economic evolution. You're part of it. And how you move forward will, quite literally, help shape what comes next.

At its essence, *Mission-Driven Money* is about wholeness. It urges us to close the unnatural divide between commerce and conscience, between financial gain and personal meaning. Drawing from fields as diverse as behavioural science, economics, and real-world enterprise, it makes the case that purpose is not fluff—it's fuel. You'll see how purpose catalyses performance, how impact can be monetised without diluting integrity, and how entrepreneurs can build ventures that are both durable and deeply aligned with their values.

You'll encounter frameworks such as the Mission-Mapping Blueprint and the Burnout Barometer—tools designed not just to inspire but to ground your ambition in clarity and alignment. You'll read stories of founders who've defied conventional definitions of success and charted new, more fulfilling paths. And you'll be asked—gently, but persistently—to reflect on your own motivations, decisions, and what you hope to leave behind.

This isn't a tidy, step-by-step instruction manual. Life rarely is. Instead, think of it as an exploration—rich, layered, sometimes contradictory—of what it really means to flourish in an age where meaning is no longer optional. It acknowledges the tension between striving and stillness, ambition and authenticity. It won't pretend that the journey is easy. But it will insist, again and again, that it's worth it.

We are, after all, in an age that demands more from its leaders—more nuance, more heart, more moral courage. The challenges we face—environmental collapse, inequality, societal unrest—require more than just clever business models. They require a new kind of leadership: one that is as focused on conscience as it is on capital. Those who are mission-driven have a critical role to play—not just as entrepreneurs or executives, but as stewards of a better version of capitalism. This book exists to support that role.

So here you are. At a threshold. On one side lies the familiar road: status, scale, accolades. On the other, a more uncertain but far richer route—where money follows meaning, where work becomes a vessel for purpose, and where success feels not just impressive, but right. This isn't idealism. It's a viable, actionable framework for those ready to lead with both ambition and soul.

The question isn't whether you *can* integrate purpose and profit. The question is—will you?

Chapter 1
The Myth of Passion vs. Profit

We've all heard the refrain: "Follow your passion and the money will follow." It's practically gospel in modern motivational culture—tossed around in graduation speeches, business podcasts, and coffee-table manifestos on personal fulfilment. There's a seductive simplicity to it, a promise that if you just do what you love, the rest will fall into place. But that tidy narrative—however charming—is incomplete. In truth, it borders on dangerous. For many, this mantra has become less a guiding light and more a mirage, luring them into cycles of frustration, burnout, and financial instability.

This chapter aims to pull back the curtain on the passion myth, not to diminish the importance of doing work you care about, but to frame it in sharper, more grounded terms. Because while passion is undeniably powerful—a kind of emotional rocket fuel—it's not a standalone GPS for building a meaningful, sustainable livelihood. The idea that passion alone is enough to carry you through the rigours of entrepreneurship or career building is, frankly, romantic at best and reckless at worst. What's needed now is a more integrated lens—one that honours emotion but anchors it in structure, foresight, and value creation.

The root of the problem lies in a basic confusion: we often mistake emotional intensity for long-term direction. Passion is, by its nature, volatile. It burns brightly but erratically. People often launch into new ventures fired up by an idea, a calling, a cause. And initially, that ignition matters. But soon enough, reality arrives—with its spreadsheets, customer complaints, hiring dilemmas, supply chain issues. The logistics of actually running something—be it a business or a career—rarely feel "passionate." And yet, those are the very mechanisms that turn intention into impact, and effort into income.

What's more, this inflated reverence for passion puts many in an odd kind of bind. If you're not waking up thrilled each morning, the assumption is that you must be on the wrong path. This expectation—of constant emotional high—can be subtly corrosive. It encourages people to abandon meaningful endeavours the moment they become routine, or worse, difficult. Particularly in purpose-driven work, where the payoff is often delayed, and the emotional labour immense, relying on passion as your only engine is a recipe for burnout. Enthusiasm without architecture crumbles under pressure. To build something lasting, you need more than momentum—you need scaffolding.

If we step back and look at the broader picture, the tension between money and meaning is nothing new. Throughout human history, wealth has always been a proxy—not the goal itself, but a stand-in for deeper yearnings: safety, recognition, belonging, legacy. We've never really wanted money for its own sake, have we? What we're after is the freedom it can afford, the influence it confers, the story it allows us to tell about who we are and what we value.

This view is supported by decades of research. Positive psychology and behavioural economics both tell us the same thing: once basic needs and a degree of comfort are met, additional income has diminishing returns on happiness. But how the money is earned—now that's a different story. Studies suggest that meaning-rich work continues to boost well-being long after the novelty of a pay rise fades.

One landmark study, led by psychologists Tim Kasser and Richard Ryan, found that individuals who orient their lives around intrinsic goals—things like personal growth, community contribution, authentic connection—report significantly higher life satisfaction than those chasing external rewards like status or wealth. Neuroscience, too, adds an intriguing layer here. Intrinsic motivation lights up brain regions tied to long-term reward and deep engagement, while extrinsic drivers, like bonuses or praise, deliver quick hits of dopamine—pleasurable but fleeting. The result? A perpetual hunger for the next "win," without ever feeling truly full.

This difference—between performance and purpose—is more than academic. It's foundational. Purpose, when rightly understood, is about congruence. It's the alignment between what you believe, what you do, and the effect you have on others. Performance, especially in today's metrics-obsessed culture, can too easily become a chase for visibility, applause, scale. Combine the two, however, and something potent emerges. You move from simply "doing work" to embodying it. Your job becomes an extension of your values, not a departure from them.

Take Sarah Kauss, for example—the founder of S'well. Her journey didn't start with a grandiose business plan. It began with a conviction: to reduce single-use plastic and promote sustainability. That purpose, married with her interest in product design, became the foundation of a company now worth over $100 million. But what powered her success wasn't passion in isolation—it was her ability to translate that passion into a business model rooted in operational clarity, smart branding, and responsiveness to market needs. It's this kind of synergy—values informing venture—that defines mission-led wealth.

Or consider Hamdi Ulukaya, the man behind Chobani. His story—an immigrant starting a yoghurt brand in a saturated market—shouldn't have been a winning one. But Ulukaya's mission was never just about dairy. It was about people. He built his company on a commitment to equity: hiring refugees, sharing profits, creating inclusive workplaces. The result? Chobani didn't just thrive—it became a template for how companies can lead with conscience and still compete at the highest levels. Ulukaya's principles weren't a liability; they were his edge.

What links stories like Kauss's and Ulukaya's isn't mere enthusiasm. It's the ability to operationalise belief. These are individuals who didn't just feel strongly about something—they built systems around those feelings. They understood that intention must be paired with execution. Purpose became their differentiator, and business acumen their amplifier.

If you're reading this with a sense of longing or curiosity—wondering how to bring your own work into greater alignment—you're not alone. The first step isn't to chase a flash of inspiration. It's to interrogate what sits beneath it. What irritates you about the world? What problem do you feel absurdly compelled to solve? What would you stick with, even if it wasn't glamorous or fast-moving? These aren't idle musings. They're directional tools. They help you move beyond the sugar rush of excitement into the steadier terrain of devotion.

This chapter doesn't just offer ideas—it provides a toolkit. You'll engage with exercises designed to help clarify your core motivations, sift superficial enthusiasm from enduring mission, and map your values onto real-world market needs. This isn't about choosing between purpose and profit—it's about engineering a structure where they support one another.

The notion that you must choose between making a living and making a difference is outdated, and frankly, a bit lazy. That binary has outlived its usefulness. It's time we replaced it with something more dynamic—an entrepreneurial model that insists on depth, that rewards coherence, that understands money not as a rival to meaning, but as its capable ally.

In the pages ahead, you'll discover how to shift from vague yearning to clear strategy, how to channel your values into enterprise, and how to create a career or business that doesn't ask you to sever yourself in two. Passion might get you started. But it's purpose, married to structure, that will keep the fire burning. So, shall we begin?

The Passion Trap: Why Following Your Bliss Alone Won't Pay the Bills

Few ideas have infiltrated the modern imagination more deeply than the notion that passion is the key to success. Popularised in everything from graduation speeches to bestselling self-help books, the belief that one must "follow their bliss" in order to live a fulfilling and financially rewarding life has become cultural dogma. It sounds empowering, even liberating. But when held up to the demands of reality, it quickly reveals its limitations. Passion, without structure, strategy, and sustainable systems, is often not a pathway to success—but a detour that leads many into emotional exhaustion and financial instability.

This is not to dismiss passion outright. It plays a vital role in sparking interest, fuelling creativity, and driving initial momentum. But the notion that passion alone is enough has proven to be not only misleading but actively harmful to many well-intentioned individuals. What makes the passion trap so insidious is precisely its surface-level appeal. It encourages people to prioritise emotional intensity over practical viability, to pursue projects based on how they feel rather than how they function. In the absence of a deeper purpose and a grounded business model, what begins as enthusiasm often ends in burnout.

The danger of this seductive ideal becomes clear when we consider the number of people who have left stable careers to pursue passion projects, only to find themselves overwhelmed by the financial and operational realities of entrepreneurship. Take, for instance, the wave of professionals who exited corporate roles during the rise of the "great resignation," inspired by the promise of meaningful work on their own terms. Many launched small businesses centred around their interests—artisanal baking, holistic coaching, craft design—only to discover within a year that passion didn't pay the rent, attract customers, or replace the infrastructure they had once taken for granted. According to research published by the Bureau of Labor Statistics and supported by analysis from Harvard Business Review, roughly 20% of small businesses fail in their first year, and nearly half don't survive past the fifth. A significant contributing factor is the lack of strategic planning beyond the founder's initial enthusiasm.

Part of the issue is semantic. Passion is often mistaken for purpose, yet the two are fundamentally different. Passion is about what excites you; purpose is about what endures. Passion is emotional; purpose is directional. Passion may tell you what you love doing, but purpose tells you *why* it matters—to others, not just to yourself. Without this outward orientation, passion becomes self-referential. It fuels performance in bursts but offers little guidance when challenges arise or when enthusiasm wanes. Purpose, by contrast, is grounded in contribution. It provides the resilience and clarity needed to navigate complexity and sustain effort over time.

Research in psychology and behavioural science further substantiates this distinction. A 2019 study published in the journal *Motivation and Emotion* found that people who pursued goals driven by intrinsic values (those related to meaning and service) experienced greater long-term satisfaction and lower levels of burnout than those who pursued goals rooted solely in personal enjoyment or self-expression. Similarly, the work of Daniel Pink, particularly in *Drive: The Surprising Truth About What Motivates Us*, reveals that mastery, autonomy, and purpose are the true engines of sustained motivation—not fleeting emotional highs.

Moreover, from a neuroscientific perspective, the pursuit of passion often activates the brain's dopaminergic reward system in a way that mirrors addictive behaviour. The early stages of a new venture or creative project feel thrilling because of the novelty and reward anticipation. However, as the dopamine spike subsides and the inevitable difficulties surface, motivation drops sharply—especially when there is no deeper "why" to sustain it. Without a clearly articulated purpose, many individuals find themselves chasing the next high, moving from project to project in a restless cycle of pursuit and disappointment.

Contrast this with the experience of those who ground their work in a clear mission. Consider the example of Scott Harrison, founder of charity: water. Harrison left a lucrative career in nightlife promotion—an industry driven almost entirely by image and superficial passion—to dedicate himself to solving the global water crisis. What began as a personal reckoning quickly transformed into one of the most impactful non-profits of the 21st century, bringing clean water to over 15 million people. Harrison's work is not fuelled by passion alone; it is anchored in a mission that transcends personal satisfaction. And that mission has allowed him to endure the rigours of fundraising, public scrutiny, and organisational leadership with uncommon perseverance.

The key insight here is not that passion is irrelevant, but that it must be channelled through purpose and supported by strategic execution. Purpose introduces constraints, and while that may sound counterintuitive in a culture that idolises freedom, constraints are precisely what allow for creativity to become productive. Without them, passion becomes a kind of chaos—exciting, yes, but ultimately unsustainable.

This has direct implications for those attempting to build mission-driven businesses. The most successful social entrepreneurs do not start with the question, "What do I love to do?" but rather, "What problem am I willing to solve, even when it's hard?" Passion may help identify areas of interest, but it is purpose that identifies needs—and therein lies the economic value. People pay for problems to be solved. Markets respond to value, not enthusiasm. The most effective way to turn passion into profit is to align what you love with what others need, and to build a structure that supports delivering that value consistently over time.

This alignment can be seen in the story of Sara Blakely, the founder of Spanx. Blakely was not "passionate" about shapewear in the romanticised sense. She didn't dream of hosiery as a child. What she did have was a persistent frustration with existing products, an acute understanding of consumer pain points, and the drive to create a better solution. Her passion emerged from her purpose, not the other way around. Her commitment to solving a real problem with empathy, grit, and ingenuity led to the creation of a billion-dollar brand—without outside investment. Her story exemplifies how meaningful impact and financial success intersect when purpose guides the business, and passion is used as fuel rather than compass.

So how does one avoid falling into the passion trap? The answer lies in cultivating what philosopher Angela Duckworth terms "grit"—the combination of passion and perseverance directed toward long-term goals. Grit is not about raw enthusiasm but about the disciplined pursuit of purpose over time. It is about showing up, especially when the novelty wears off. It involves clarifying values, building systems, testing assumptions, and iterating constantly. It is not glamorous, but it is transformative.

Practically speaking, this requires reframing how we think about passion. Instead of treating it as a fixed trait to be discovered, we must see it as a dynamic energy that can be developed and refined in alignment with purpose. This means being willing to interrogate our motivations, experiment with different forms of contribution, and build feedback loops that help us identify where our strengths meet real-world demand. It also means recognising that fulfilment often follows mastery—that deep satisfaction is rarely immediate, but is cultivated through meaningful effort over time.

Ultimately, the passion trap is a cautionary tale about the dangers of mistaking intensity for intention. It warns us against building our lives and livelihoods on emotional surges without grounding them in strategy, service, and sustainability. Passion can start the fire, but purpose keeps it burning. By understanding the distinction—and by learning to harmonise emotional drive with thoughtful design—we create the conditions for work that is not only personally meaningful but also economically viable.

This is the ethos that underpins mission-driven money. It is not a rejection of passion, but a demand that it be integrated with purpose and guided by wisdom. For those ready to move beyond temporary highs and into long-lasting impact, this shift is not just necessary—it is liberating. It replaces the anxiety of having to "find your one true passion" with the clarity of building a life around your values, your skills, and your capacity to contribute. And in doing so, it paves the way for a new kind of wealth—one that enriches not only your bank account but your entire way of being.

Money and Meaning: An Evolutionary Perspective

For much of human history, the concept of wealth was inextricably linked with survival. Long before fiat currencies, investment portfolios, or digital assets, wealth existed in the form of food stores, land ownership, and access to communal resources. To be "wealthy" meant to have what was needed to endure uncertainty, provide for kin, and contribute to the collective good. It was never solely about accumulation, but about security, status, and social cohesion. As societies evolved, the symbolic and functional dimensions of wealth expanded, yet one principle remained consistent across epochs: money, or its equivalents, derived meaning when it served a higher purpose—when it enabled not just the sustenance of life, but the shaping of it.

Modern narratives often treat money and meaning as separate, even competing forces—one rooted in pragmatism, the other in idealism. Yet when we examine both the evolutionary and psychological foundations of wealth, a more integrated story emerges. The human brain, shaped by millennia of adaptation, responds most positively not to wealth in isolation, but to wealth that is aligned with goals of purpose, contribution, and relational significance. This alignment, as research now shows, not only enhances subjective well-being but also promotes longevity, resilience, and social impact. The human desire for meaning is not a luxury of the enlightened; it is a fundamental driver of motivation encoded in our biology.

To understand this, we must first consider the evolutionary roots of value. In early hunter-gatherer societies, individuals who amassed resources purely for themselves were often ostracised or punished. Anthropological studies, such as those conducted by evolutionary biologist Christopher Boehm, reveal that egalitarianism was a central norm in many prehistoric communities. Hoarding without redistributing was seen as a threat to group cohesion and survival. Social capital—earned through cooperation, generosity, and contribution—was more enduring and valuable than material accumulation. In such environments, the most revered individuals were those who used their surplus to support others, thereby enhancing group fitness.

This early interplay between resources and meaning continues to shape modern behaviours. Today, we no longer share meat around a fire, but we do measure status through the lens of philanthropy, ethical business practices, and perceived impact. Public admiration is increasingly reserved not for those who are merely rich, but for those who use their resources with purpose. The rise of purpose-driven entrepreneurship, ethical investing, and social enterprise underscores this evolutionary continuity. We are drawn, often unconsciously, to those whose wealth carries a narrative of intention and contribution.

Psychologically, this phenomenon is supported by the theory of self-determination, developed by Edward Deci and Richard Ryan, which identifies three innate psychological needs: autonomy, competence, and relatedness. Financial resources alone do not fulfil these needs. But when wealth is directed towards goals that foster personal agency, mastery, and connection to others, it becomes a tool for psychological nourishment. Numerous studies show that individuals who use money to support causes they believe in, fund meaningful experiences, or invest in others' well-being report higher levels of happiness and life satisfaction than those who spend primarily on material goods or status symbols.

A compelling illustration of this dynamic is found in the philanthropic evolution of billionaire Chuck Feeney, co-founder of Duty Free Shoppers. Over the course of his life, Feeney secretly gave away nearly his entire fortune—over $8 billion—through his foundation, Atlantic Philanthropies. He famously lived modestly, wore a plastic watch, and avoided recognition. For Feeney, money was never the goal; it was a mechanism for achieving large-scale change in health, education, and human rights. His life's work reframes wealth not as a destination, but as an instrument of mission. The result? A legacy celebrated not for excess, but for impact.

Another example lies in the world of social entrepreneurship. TOMS, the shoe company founded by Blake Mycoskie, was built on a model of "one for one"—for every pair of shoes sold, a pair was donated to a child in need. While the business model later evolved in response to critiques about long-term development efficacy, the brand's initial explosive growth highlighted the consumer appetite for products that combine financial value with social good. For millions of customers, purchasing TOMS was not just a transaction; it was a statement of values. It exemplified how meaning amplifies economic behaviour, creating a feedback loop of purpose-driven commerce.

From a biological standpoint, this alignment between money and meaning has measurable effects on human health. A 2016 study published in *Proceedings of the National Academy of Sciences* found that individuals with a strong sense of purpose in life had lower risks of cardiovascular disease, cognitive decline, and premature mortality. Purpose, it appears, has protective effects not just psychologically, but physiologically. When people feel that their work and their resources are contributing to something larger than themselves, their stress levels diminish, their immune systems strengthen, and their cognitive resilience improves. In essence, meaning is not only good for the soul—it is good for the body.

This insight has profound implications for how we think about wealth creation. It challenges the dominant narrative that financial success must be fuelled by competition, urgency, and self-interest. Instead, it proposes a model where strategic financial growth can be harmonised with psychological flourishing. This does not mean that mission-driven individuals must reject profit or view money with suspicion. On the contrary, it encourages them to embrace wealth as a legitimate and powerful extension of their values—a resource that, when used wisely, can expand their ability to serve, create, and influence.

There are also practical applications for entrepreneurs and leaders. Structuring a business around a clear mission can enhance employee engagement, customer loyalty, and investor interest. Companies like Patagonia, Ben & Jerry's, and Warby Parker have shown that when a brand's financial goals are transparently tied to social or environmental missions, they outperform competitors in both resilience and reputation. These companies are not successful *despite* their values—they are successful *because* of them. They tap into the deep human need to belong to something meaningful, offering customers and employees alike a sense of identity and alignment.

This orientation also changes how individuals approach financial planning on a personal level. Rather than saving or investing out of fear or scarcity, people who link their financial goals to a meaningful life vision report higher levels of discipline, optimism, and fulfilment. Financial planners who integrate purpose-based coaching into their practice often find that clients make better decisions, experience less anxiety, and remain more committed to long-term strategies. Wealth, when framed as a tool to support a values-driven life, becomes far less stressful and far more energising.

It is important to note that this approach does not romanticise poverty or negate the importance of material security. Basic financial stability is essential for human functioning. But once those needs are met, the pursuit of more money for its own sake tends to yield diminishing psychological returns. Meaning, however, continues to compound. It deepens with time, grows with service, and spreads through influence. When wealth is used to further a mission—whether personal, communal, or global—it extends its impact beyond the ledger and into the legacy one leaves behind.

Ultimately, what this evolutionary and psychological lens reveals is that wealth, like fire, is neither inherently good nor bad. Its value lies in how it is used. When directed toward self-aggrandisement or hoarding, it isolates. When shared, invested in purpose, and aligned with contribution, it connects and transforms. It becomes the fuel not only for a comfortable life, but for a meaningful one.

As we rethink the relationship between money and meaning, we are invited to challenge a critical assumption: that financial success and moral integrity are mutually exclusive. History, science, and lived experience all suggest otherwise. The most enduring wealth is not measured by balance sheets, but by impact. And in a world increasingly hungry for authenticity, integrity, and purpose, there has never been a more compelling time to align what we earn with what we stand for.

Purpose vs. Performance: What Really Drives Sustainable Success?

What fuels sustained excellence? Is it the pressure of performance metrics, the lure of external rewards, or something deeper and more enduring? This question sits at the centre of debates in behavioural economics, neuroscience, and leadership theory, and its implications are profound—not just for individuals seeking meaningful careers, but for organisations aspiring to long-term success.

In an era dominated by data, deliverables, and productivity dashboards, it's easy to assume that high performance stems from well-structured incentive systems. From quarterly bonuses to accolades, from promotions to public recognition, the machinery of modern work is designed to optimise output through rewards. Yet a growing body of interdisciplinary research reveals a more complex picture—one that calls into question the sustainability of extrinsically driven performance. The emerging consensus suggests that the most enduring form of success arises not from external validation but from an internal sense of purpose. And when that purpose is properly cultivated, it can outperform even the most carefully engineered incentive structures.

At the heart of this insight lies the distinction between *intrinsic* and *extrinsic* motivation. Intrinsic motivation refers to the drive to engage in an activity for its inherent satisfaction—for the joy of problem-solving, the challenge of mastery, or the fulfilment of contribution. Extrinsic motivation, by contrast, depends on outcomes separate from the activity itself, such as money, recognition, or avoidance of punishment. The difference between the two may seem academic, but its consequences for behaviour, creativity, resilience, and long-term fulfilment are anything but.

Behavioural economist Dan Ariely has explored this dynamic extensively in his work on motivation and meaning. In one of his most cited experiments, participants were asked to complete a repetitive task—assembling Lego figures—under different reward conditions. In one version, the assembled figures were kept intact; in the other, they were disassembled in front of the participant as soon as they were completed. Despite being offered the same monetary reward, participants in the second condition were far less motivated to continue. The takeaway was clear: when people sense that their efforts are futile or disconnected from a meaningful purpose, even financial incentives cannot sustain engagement.

Neuroscience provides a complementary perspective. Functional MRI studies have shown that intrinsically motivated tasks activate the mesolimbic dopamine system—the same pathway involved in feelings of pleasure and reward. However, when an activity becomes overly associated with external rewards, this neural response can diminish. The phenomenon, known as the "overjustification effect," explains why people sometimes lose interest in activities they once enjoyed once those activities become monetised or externally evaluated. The brain begins to code the task not as inherently rewarding, but as instrumental—and once the external reward is removed or diminished, so too is the motivation.

This insight holds particular significance for entrepreneurs and mission-driven professionals, whose work often sits at the intersection of ambition and impact. While financial rewards are important—and indeed, necessary for sustainability—they are insufficient to carry individuals through the inevitable setbacks, uncertainties, and sacrifices involved in building something meaningful. Purpose, by contrast, acts as a stabilising force. It is what allows individuals to persist when results are slow, recognition is sparse, and pressure is high.

Consider the case of Muhammad Yunus, the founder of Grameen Bank and pioneer of microfinance. Long before the concept gained international traction, Yunus began offering small loans to impoverished women in rural Bangladesh—not for personal gain, but because he believed access to capital was a basic human right. His motivation was not to build a banking empire but to solve a systemic injustice. Yet the ripple effects of his purpose-driven approach transformed the global development landscape, earning him a Nobel Peace Prize and influencing policies across continents. Yunus's impact was not the result of performance targets, but of unwavering commitment to a mission. His success—both financial and societal—was a by-product of purpose.

Contrast this with high-profile cases of extrinsically fuelled burnout in the corporate world. The implosion of companies like Theranos or the ethical scandals that plagued Enron and Wells Fargo illustrate the dangers of prioritising performance over purpose. In these environments, short-term metrics overshadowed long-term integrity. Employees, incentivised to meet targets at all costs, engaged in unethical behaviour or pushed themselves beyond sustainable limits. The absence of a unifying ethical mission created cultures where performance became divorced from meaning—and where success, though measurable in the short term, ultimately proved hollow.

The business world is beginning to internalise these lessons. Companies that centre purpose—not just in their branding, but in their operational DNA—are attracting better talent, retaining employees longer, and performing more consistently over time. Research from Deloitte and EY shows that purpose-driven organisations outperform their peers in financial performance and employee engagement. Importantly, the data suggests that purpose is not a soft, feel-good abstraction. It is a strategic asset, capable of enhancing productivity, innovation, and resilience.

On an individual level, this insight invites a deeper interrogation of what truly sustains high performance. In coaching environments, elite performers—whether in sport, business, or the arts—often speak not of trophies or salaries, but of alignment. They refer to the sense of flow that comes when their daily work reflects their deeper values. This concept of "flow," originally introduced by psychologist Mihaly Csikszentmihalyi, refers to a state of intense, immersive engagement in which challenge and skill are perfectly balanced. Flow is more likely to emerge in tasks driven by intrinsic motivation, and it is strongly correlated with peak performance and well-being.

Purpose is the context that gives rise to flow. It provides a narrative arc that makes difficult tasks feel worthwhile and setbacks feel meaningful. Without it, even success can feel empty—accomplishment without coherence. A landmark longitudinal study conducted by Yale University's Amy Wrzesniewski found that individuals who viewed their work as a calling—not merely a job or career—reported significantly higher job satisfaction, lower stress levels, and greater commitment. Crucially, they also tended to be more productive and more innovative. Again, we see the interplay between meaning and measurable outcomes: purpose drives performance not by replacing metrics, but by giving them context.

This does not mean that performance metrics should be abandoned. On the contrary, tracking progress is essential for accountability and growth. But those metrics must be nested within a framework of values. When performance is tethered to purpose, it becomes sustainable. When it is detached, it becomes extractive. Leaders, therefore, must not only articulate a compelling mission but must also design systems and cultures that reinforce that mission at every level—from incentives to communication to strategic decision-making.

The integration of purpose and performance also changes how we think about setbacks. In a purpose-driven paradigm, failure is not merely a deviation from expected results; it is an opportunity for learning and recalibration. This mindset reduces fear-based behaviours and encourages experimentation—hallmarks of innovative and adaptive organisations. It also builds resilience, as individuals are more likely to persist in the face of difficulty when they believe in the significance of their work. Carol Dweck's research on growth mindset further supports this: those who see challenges as part of a meaningful process, rather than as threats to their status, are more likely to thrive over time.

In practical terms, cultivating purpose in a high-performance environment requires intentional effort. It begins with asking questions that often get lost in the rush of deliverables: Why does this work matter? Who does it serve? What long-term good does it create? These questions are not philosophical luxuries—they are strategic imperatives. They shape how individuals prioritise, how teams collaborate, and how organisations evolve.

As the future of work continues to shift—towards remote structures, flexible roles, and decentralised leadership—the need for intrinsic anchors becomes even more pronounced. Without the traditional scaffolding of office culture or hierarchical oversight, individuals must rely more heavily on self-direction and internal motivation. In this context, purpose is not just beneficial—it is indispensable.

The lesson from behavioural economics and neuroscience is clear: human beings are not machines optimised by rewards alone. We are meaning-makers, constantly seeking coherence between our actions and our identity. Sustainable success arises when performance serves a purpose that resonates with our values and aspirations. This is not a trade-off—it is an alignment. And it is this alignment that allows us to not only perform at our best, but to do so in a way that is emotionally sustainable, ethically grounded, and socially impactful.

In the final analysis, the most powerful performance driver is not the promise of reward or the threat of failure—it is the deep, often quiet conviction that what we are doing matters. When that conviction is present, success becomes not a fleeting high, but a grounded state of contribution. And in that state, both individuals and organisations find their most enduring edge.

The Power of Alignment: Finding Your 'Why' Beyond Money

In a world increasingly shaped by rapid change and persistent uncertainty, clarity of purpose has become one of the most valuable forms of capital. Beyond qualifications, connections, and even capital itself, what ultimately distinguishes those who thrive from those who stagnate is a clear sense of alignment—a deep-rooted understanding of *why* they do what they do. This 'why' is not a slogan, a marketing tagline, or a vague aspiration. It is a central organising principle that guides decisions, energises action, and integrates one's emotional and financial life into a cohesive whole.

Yet finding this sense of purpose—especially beyond the conventional metrics of success—can be surprisingly elusive. Many individuals, even those who are outwardly successful, find themselves grappling with internal dissatisfaction, unsure whether the work they do truly reflects who they are. This misalignment between action and intention, between money earned and meaning felt, is not just a philosophical inconvenience. It is a source of chronic stress, decision fatigue, and a subtle erosion of motivation over time.

The solution lies not in abandoning the pursuit of financial wealth, but in reconnecting that pursuit with something more personal and enduring. Purpose-driven alignment does not reject material ambition; rather, it places money in service of something deeper. It allows for success that is not only sustainable but fulfilling—

because it emerges from congruence between what matters to us and what we do every day.

The concept of alignment has strong roots in both psychology and business. From the perspective of humanistic psychology, alignment is closely tied to the idea of self-actualisation—a state in which an individual's actions, beliefs, and desires are harmonised. Abraham Maslow, whose hierarchy of needs is widely referenced in motivational theory, suggested that the pinnacle of human development lies in expressing one's true self in a meaningful way. Interestingly, Maslow's later writings, often overlooked, placed *self-transcendence*—contributing to something beyond the self—even above self-actualisation. In other words, purpose is not just about inner fulfilment; it's also about outward impact.

Neuroscience reinforces this perspective. Studies on brain function reveal that when individuals engage in activities that align with their values and intrinsic goals, their prefrontal cortex—responsible for planning, decision-making, and social behaviour—becomes more active. This facilitates better judgement, increased focus, and a higher tolerance for setbacks. Purpose, it turns out, is not just motivational fluff—it is neurologically beneficial, enhancing cognitive performance and emotional regulation.

Yet, for many, finding this 'why' beyond money remains an abstract or intimidating exercise. Part of the problem is that conventional career guidance tends to be either overly prescriptive or too vague, offering platitudes rather than practical pathways. Real alignment requires a more reflective, structured, and personal approach. It is not something that appears fully formed after reading a book or attending a workshop. It is uncovered through deliberate introspection, behavioural experimentation, and honest feedback from the environments in which we live and work.

One powerful method for uncovering personal alignment is through what can be called values excavation. This involves identifying not just what you enjoy doing, but what you *feel compelled* to address in the world. These are often issues or needs that consistently evoke strong emotional responses—anger at injustice, deep empathy for others, or excitement about solving certain types of problems. Values are often revealed not by our goals, but by our *frustrations*—the moments when we feel most dissonant, when we say to ourselves, "This isn't how things should be."

Take the example of Leila Janah, founder of Samasource, a social enterprise dedicated to providing dignified digital work to people living in poverty. Janah's work was not born from a desire to build a company, but from a visceral dissatisfaction with the charity model she encountered while working in developing countries. Her sense of injustice regarding how talent was overlooked due to geography fuelled her determination to create an alternative. That alignment between her emotional values and professional direction enabled her to build a multimillion-dollar enterprise that changed thousands of lives. Her 'why' was not abstract—it was activated, embodied, and continuously refined through experience.

Another practical approach to finding alignment is narrative reframing—examining your life not as a series of disconnected events, but as a coherent story in which certain patterns and themes reveal a deeper purpose. What types of challenges have you repeatedly returned to? Where have you found fulfilment that defied expectations? What roles—mentor, builder, advocate, creator—do you naturally gravitate toward, even when they're not rewarded? These questions help trace the outlines of a personal mission that transcends fleeting interests or market trends.

It is also essential to separate true alignment from performative or inherited ambition. Many people mistake socially rewarded behaviours for personal purpose. They chase what looks meaningful to others, rather than what resonates internally. The disconnection that results can be subtle at first—feeling uninspired despite achieving goals, or craving change without understanding why. But over time, this kind of misalignment erodes engagement and, eventually, self-trust.

Authentic alignment, by contrast, tends to produce a paradoxical effect: it feels both grounding and expansive. Grounding because it affirms who you are; expansive because it reveals how your unique perspective can contribute to something larger than yourself. It connects financial goals to human significance, enabling wealth to be not just a measure of output but a medium of influence.

This becomes especially powerful when turned into practical strategy. Entrepreneurs who operate with alignment tend to build businesses that reflect their deepest convictions. Their brand is not a mask, but a mirror. Consider Yvon Chouinard, founder of Patagonia, who famously declared, "I never wanted to be a businessman." His alignment with environmental activism shaped every aspect of the company—from its supply chain ethics to its political advocacy—and ultimately led to the extraordinary decision to transfer company ownership to a trust that supports climate causes. His wealth became a continuation of his values, not a contradiction of them.

The exercise of finding your 'why' beyond money is not only philosophical—it is intensely practical. It helps determine which opportunities to pursue, which clients to serve, and which markets to enter. It sharpens communication, simplifies branding, and clarifies pricing decisions. A business rooted in alignment will resonate more deeply with customers, attract like-minded collaborators, and weather setbacks with greater resilience.

To engage in this kind of alignment work requires a few key disciplines: consistent reflection, openness to feedback, and the courage to make countercultural choices. It may mean saying no to lucrative deals that compromise your integrity. It might involve taking the longer route to profitability in order to build something that lasts. But what it offers in return is a sense of coherence—a life where your calendar reflects your values, your income reflects your impact, and your legacy reflects who you truly are.

The final point worth emphasising is that alignment is not a fixed destination but a dynamic process. Your 'why' will evolve as you grow, as the world changes, and as your understanding of your own needs deepens. That evolution is not a sign of failure, but of maturity. Staying aligned means continually recalibrating, continually asking: Does this reflect what I believe? Am I building something that matters to me and to others? Am I using money as a tool for meaning, rather than as a substitute for it?

In the pursuit of both emotional and financial wealth, alignment is the bridge. It transforms money from a measure of effort into an expression of purpose. It ensures that success is not just achieved, but *earned*—because it resonates. And in a culture saturated with distraction and superficial benchmarks, that kind of resonance is not only rare—it is revolutionary.

Case Study: Mission-Led Millionaires

For too long, the entrepreneurial world has been divided by a false dichotomy: the idea that you can either pursue financial success or live according to your values—but not both. Traditional business thinking has often treated social impact as a cost centre, a philanthropic add-on rather than a central operating principle. Meanwhile, many purpose-driven entrepreneurs have been led to believe that to remain ethically pure, they must resist the pursuit of profit. This binary thinking is not only outdated—it is being actively disproven by a new generation of entrepreneurs who are building empires not in spite of their values, but because of them. These are the mission-led millionaires: individuals who have fused purpose with profit in ways that are both scalable and sustainable, offering proof that business can be both a tool for wealth creation and a force for good.

One of the most prominent examples of this integration is Jessica Alba, actress-turned-entrepreneur and co-founder of The Honest Company. Frustrated by the lack of transparency and safety in children's products, Alba launched the business in 2012 with a mission to offer ethically made, non-toxic household and baby goods. The company's values—environmental responsibility, ingredient integrity, and ethical supply chains—were not tacked on as a marketing strategy; they were embedded in its DNA. Within just a few years, The Honest Company became a billion-dollar brand, gaining customer loyalty not merely through aesthetic appeal or clever advertising, but through a genuine alignment with rising consumer demand for safe, values-driven products.

What distinguishes Alba's venture is not just its growth, but the way it demonstrates the strategic advantage of mission clarity. Consumers, particularly millennials and Gen Z, are increasingly choosing brands that reflect their values. In a marketplace flooded with options, purpose becomes a differentiator. Alba's success underscores a vital truth: values are not liabilities—they are assets, capable of enhancing brand equity, driving innovation, and fostering trust in an era of corporate scepticism.

Another compelling case is that of John Mackey, co-founder of Whole Foods Market. Long before "organic" and "sustainable" became mainstream buzzwords, Mackey was building a business rooted in conscious capitalism—a philosophy that prioritises the well-being of all stakeholders, not just shareholders. Whole Foods began as a small natural foods store in Austin, Texas, but its mission to change the way people eat and live attracted a loyal customer base and a passionate workforce. Even when the company faced scrutiny over pricing or its eventual acquisition by Amazon, its foundational values continued to guide decisions and shape public perception. Mackey's career demonstrates that profitability and ethical leadership can not only coexist but thrive in tandem, provided that the commitment to purpose is authentic and unwavering.

Then there is the story of Adi Tatarko and Alon Cohen, the Israeli-American couple who founded Houzz, a platform that revolutionised the home renovation and design industry. While their initial motivation was deeply personal—stemming from their own frustrating experience renovating a home—their approach to business was anything but casual. They recognised that homeowners, designers, and contractors all needed a more transparent, accessible, and collaborative platform. What began as a passion project quickly scaled into a tech company valued at over $4 billion. Their mission to democratise good design and empower creative professionals shaped the platform's evolution and community-first ethos. In this case, values fuelled innovation, which in turn fuelled revenue. The couple's journey reveals how personal mission, when paired with digital strategy and market insight, can catalyse extraordinary growth.

Social entrepreneurship offers another fertile ground for mission-led wealth creation. One standout figure in this space is Meagan Fallone, former CEO of Barefoot College, an organisation that trains rural women—many of them grandmothers—in solar engineering and entrepreneurial skills. The initiative has reached dozens of countries and impacted tens of thousands of lives. While Barefoot College operates as a non-profit, Fallone's leadership transformed its approach to scale, partnerships, and sustainability, turning it into a globally recognised model for community-led development. Her work exemplifies how business acumen, when married to moral clarity, can produce results that outperform many for-profit ventures in terms of long-term impact.

A particularly instructive case is that of Yvon Chouinard, the founder of Patagonia, whose radical commitment to environmental activism has redefined what it means to be a mission-led entrepreneur. Chouinard built a thriving outdoor apparel company while challenging the very foundations of consumer culture. Patagonia's policies—such as its "Don't Buy This Jacket" campaign, product repair services, and annual donation of 1% of sales to environmental causes—reflect a philosophy that values ecological stewardship over limitless expansion. And yet, the company continues to grow, not despite its values, but because of them. Patagonia's brand loyalty is legendary, and its financial performance continues to outpace many competitors. Chouinard's decision in 2022 to transfer ownership of the company to a trust that funds environmental causes only deepened public trust and cemented his legacy as a pioneer of ethical capitalism.

What unites these diverse entrepreneurs is a shared refusal to accept the trade-off between doing good and doing well. They have each demonstrated that purpose can be operationalised—that it can inform hiring practices, product development, customer engagement, and leadership decisions in ways that enhance both moral integrity and financial performance. These individuals did not treat values as a side project. Instead, they embedded them into their organisations at every level, from strategic vision to supply chain management.

Importantly, these stories also challenge the stereotype of the mission-led entrepreneur as someone operating on the financial margins, sustained only by idealism. These are not hobbyists or naïve do-gooders. They are skilled operators, innovative thinkers, and strategic decision-makers who understand that impact and income are not competing goals, but complementary outcomes. Their ventures are not immune to pressure, competition, or setbacks—but their clarity of purpose enables them to respond to challenges with greater agility and conviction.

From a behavioural economics perspective, the success of mission-led millionaires is consistent with what research tells us about human motivation and consumer behaviour. People are not solely driven by price and utility; they are deeply influenced by trust, identity, and values alignment. When businesses tap into these deeper drivers, they create emotional loyalty, which is far more resilient than transactional relationships. Neuroscientific studies on trust and reward reinforce this point, showing that the brain's reward systems are more strongly activated when individuals engage in purpose-aligned actions—whether as consumers, employees, or founders.

For aspiring entrepreneurs, these case studies offer more than inspiration—they offer a strategic roadmap. They suggest that the most important early-stage asset is not capital, but clarity. What problem are you uniquely positioned to solve? What values are you unwilling to compromise? How can your business model reflect and reinforce your mission rather than dilute it? These are not soft questions—they are hard-edged strategic decisions that shape hiring, pricing, product design, and growth trajectories.

They also serve as a counter-narrative to the hyper-competitive, burnout-prone culture of hustle for hustle's sake. By building ventures around deeply held convictions, mission-led millionaires are not only creating wealth—they are creating alignment between their inner lives and outer achievements. This kind of congruence is rare in business, and it is increasingly what customers, employees, and investors are seeking.

The rise of mission-led millionaires does not signal a departure from capitalism, but a reinvention of it. It reveals that markets can reward purpose when it is authentic, strategic, and woven into the very fabric of a company. It proves that values are not just nice to have—they are profitable. And it reminds us that the most enduring ventures are not those that pursue money alone, but those that understand money as a means to amplify meaning.

Chapter 2
The Psychology of Purpose-Driven Wealth

We inhabit an age where motivation, more than time or even talent, functions as a kind of modern-day currency—arguably the most valuable asset in the entrepreneurial toolkit. And yet, for those whose work is rooted in mission and meaning, staying motivated in the pursuit of financial growth can feel strangely at odds with their deeper impulses. There's a quiet tension: they want to build lives—and businesses—that stand for something, but end up drained by endless decision-making, ensnared in limiting beliefs about money, or simply demoralised when their financial reality fails to reflect their efforts. Why does this happen? To answer that, we must look beneath the surface tactics and peer into the psychological machinery that governs motivation itself.

This chapter ventures into that inner architecture, tracing the contours of purpose-driven wealth through insights from neuroscience, behavioural economics, and the psychology of performance. We'll challenge the tired assumption that meaning and money live on separate planes. In fact, when tethered to intrinsic motivation, wealth creation becomes not only sustainable but also deeply rewarding on a psychological level. Purpose, then, isn't some vague ideal floated by optimists—it's a neurological advantage, a structural support for resilience, clarity, and consistent effort that extrinsic incentives alone rarely deliver.

At the centre of this conversation is dopamine—the neurotransmitter that underwrites our drive. Pop culture tends to cast dopamine as a kind of hedonist's chemical, the stuff of fleeting highs. But its true role is more nuanced. Dopamine isn't primarily about reward itself; rather, it's about the chase. It motivates us not through the pleasure of attainment, but through the anticipation of something meaningful just beyond the horizon. In this way, mission-aligned financial goals can sustain engagement far more effectively than generic incentives—because they register as emotionally relevant, even personal.

When we're fuelled by a cause that matters, each incremental win—however modest—feeds that dopaminergic cycle. The result is not a quick thrill but a reinforcing loop of motivation, one that keeps the wheels turning even when results are slow to arrive. This is especially crucial in entrepreneurship, where the road is long, and the markers of progress can be frustratingly spaced out. Purpose offers a stabilising mechanism: a narrative that renders the grind worthwhile. Strip that away, and what's left is a fragile system, where motivation runs on novelty and crumbles under repetition.

Still, even the most values-driven individuals are not immune to the cognitive traps that derail performance. Chief among them: decision fatigue. A well-documented phenomenon in psychological literature, decision fatigue emerges when too many choices sap the brain's finite reserves of attention and willpower. For founders, creatives, and professionals navigating complex terrains, this becomes more than a nuisance—it becomes a liability. Whether it's choosing between marketing strategies, client proposals, or how to price a new product, each decision carries an emotional and cognitive cost.

Researchers Roy Baumeister and Kathleen Vohs have shown that as decision fatigue sets in, we become less capable of thinking clearly and more prone to procrastination or rash, poorly considered choices. In a purpose-led venture, this becomes doubly problematic. Because when every decision is charged with ethical or personal significance, the toll isn't just operational—it's existential. You're not just choosing a marketing tagline; you're choosing how your values show up in the world.

One way mission-led leaders cope is by reducing the volume of decisions they need to make. This isn't laziness—it's discipline. They introduce systems that shield their attention: routines, frameworks, filters. Some pare down their wardrobes or calendar structures to minimise decision friction. Others craft clear ethical guardrails or mission statements that pre-emptively answer the questions that might otherwise drain their mental energy. These systems don't inhibit creativity—they preserve it.

Equally essential to this conversation is the concept of flow, as articulated by psychologist Mihaly Csikszentmihalyi. Flow is that rare, almost sacred state of total immersion in one's work—the sweet spot where challenge and capability meet. In this state, time falls away, distractions lose their power, and output often soars. But flow doesn't occur in chaos. It arises when tasks are meaningful, goals are clear, and distractions are held at bay. In short: when work aligns with purpose.

For entrepreneurs and creatives, achieving flow is not just a perk—it's a necessity. It's the difference between pushing through the day and transcending it. And crucially, it's far more accessible when your work is animated by mission rather than metrics. Csikszentmihalyi's research confirms this: those who frequently experience flow report higher levels of life satisfaction, creativity, and long-term fulfilment. In the context of building wealth, flow isn't just about efficiency—it's a signpost of psychological congruence.

That said, even with the neurological and psychological wind at their backs, many values-driven individuals still struggle with money. Not because they're incapable of earning it, but because somewhere along the line, they absorbed a set of beliefs that frame wealth as morally suspect. Within many mission-minded communities, there lingers an implicit distrust of profit—as if money and integrity cannot coexist. The result? Underpricing. Overgiving. Avoidance of financial planning altogether. Not due to ignorance, but from a quiet fear that success will somehow compromise virtue.

Here, Carol Dweck's research on mindset provides a useful lens. While her studies focused primarily on learning, the same principles apply to money. A fixed mindset in this context sees wealth as a zero-sum game, one that casts profit as inherently extractive. An abundance mindset, by contrast, recognises money as a vehicle—a means of amplifying values and scaling impact. Those operating from this mindset don't see earning as a betrayal of their principles. They see it as a way to honour them more fully.

Shifting from scarcity to abundance is not just an intellectual exercise—it's an emotional reckoning. It requires dismantling inherited scripts about money and reimagining wealth as a resource for doing good, not a deviation from it. That's why this chapter includes a reflective exercise—the Money Mission Brainstorm—to help surface and examine these beliefs. By mapping out the emotional, relational, and societal functions of wealth, readers are invited to step into a new narrative: one where money is neither dirty nor divine, but simply a tool to be wielded with discernment.

Crucially, this is not a naïve call to optimism. It does not ignore the real-world constraints—economic, systemic, or otherwise—that many entrepreneurs face. Rather, it's a reclamation of agency. To approach wealth from a mission-driven standpoint is not to pretend that markets are fair or success guaranteed. It is to ground oneself in a psychological framework robust enough to navigate those uncertainties without fracturing under them.

Throughout this chapter, we'll continue to unpack how this inner infrastructure is built. We'll explore the science of motivation, the red flags of cognitive overload, the craft of flow-state engineering, and the undoing of inherited financial guilt. These aren't optional add-ons to the entrepreneurial skill set. They are the foundation stones of a resilient, values-aligned life.

The journey towards purpose-infused prosperity isn't about hustling harder or thinking happier thoughts. It's about developing clarity. Emotional fluency. Strategic coherence. When you integrate these elements—when your mindset and methods are stitched together by intention—then wealth becomes something more than accumulation. It becomes expression. A mirror of what matters most. This is where meaning meets money. And it starts now.

Dopamine and Drive: How Purpose Affects the Brain

In the ever-expanding conversation around motivation, dopamine is frequently cast as the biochemical protagonist—a molecular cheerleader spurring us toward our goals. But this narrative, though grounded in neuroscience, is often oversimplified. Far from being a simplistic pleasure molecule, dopamine is the neurological architecture behind drive, anticipation, and sustained effort. It governs not only what we desire, but how intensely and persistently we pursue it. And crucially, the context in which dopamine is released—the psychological meaning we attach to our goals—can radically alter the quality and sustainability of our motivation.

This has profound implications for anyone pursuing wealth, particularly mission-driven individuals who seek to align financial growth with personal values. For this group, the traditional motivators—status, competition, accumulation—often fall flat. Their ambition is fuelled less by ego and more by a desire to create impact, solve meaningful problems, and live in accordance with their beliefs. The question then becomes: can purpose act as a neurological lever, activating the brain's motivational systems in a way that supports not just fleeting enthusiasm but long-term, values-aligned financial success?

To answer that, we need to understand what dopamine actually *does*. Contrary to popular belief, dopamine is not released in greatest quantities when we receive a reward. It surges most intensely *in anticipation* of one. This makes it the neurochemical backbone of drive. It's what keeps us moving toward distant goals, even in the face of setbacks. The reward-seeking behaviour it fuels is governed by a network known as the mesolimbic pathway, which connects areas of the brain such as the ventral tegmental area (VTA), the nucleus accumbens, and the prefrontal cortex. These regions are not only involved in pleasure but in learning, decision-making, and behavioural reinforcement.

Here's where purpose enters the equation. When a goal is emotionally significant—when it resonates with our values, our identity, and our sense of meaning—the dopamine system doesn't just activate. It *optimises*. Studies have shown that people working toward goals they consider personally meaningful exhibit higher levels of dopamine-related neural activity than those working toward externally imposed or emotionally neutral goals. In other words, purpose is not a soft, spiritual concept; it is a neurological enhancer that increases the brain's capacity to stay engaged over time.

This explains why entrepreneurs with a strong mission can endure years of uncertainty, pivot through adversity, and show up with renewed energy even when immediate rewards are scarce. Their dopamine system is being fuelled not by superficial wins but by a sustained emotional investment in the *why* behind their work. This internal source of motivation is less susceptible to fatigue because it is continually reinforced by meaningful progress, however incremental. Contrast this with extrinsic motivation, which often requires ever-increasing rewards to maintain the same level of drive. Without purpose, dopamine spikes become increasingly difficult to sustain, leading to burnout, distraction, or disillusionment.

Consider the example of Blake Mycoskie, founder of TOMS. His decision to build a company based on the "one for one" model—donating a pair of shoes for every pair sold—was not just a clever marketing ploy. It was rooted in a personal experience and a clear sense of mission. The early years of TOMS were financially uncertain, but Mycoskie's emotional commitment to improving lives provided a potent source of drive. He wasn't simply building a business; he was pursuing a cause. The success that followed was not incidental—it was neuropsychologically enabled by the motivational power of purpose.

Another powerful illustration comes from Dr Paul Farmer, co-founder of Partners In Health, whose work delivering healthcare to some of the world's poorest regions is widely regarded as heroic. Operating with minimal resources, facing bureaucratic resistance and public health crises, Farmer continued for decades without the trappings of conventional success. What sustained him was not comfort or recognition but conviction. His brain was wired for the pursuit of a deeply internalised goal, which made his drive extraordinarily resilient. Though not an entrepreneur in the traditional sense, Farmer's case demonstrates how purpose can activate a form of motivation that is both neurologically robust and practically enduring.

From a practical standpoint, individuals looking to leverage the power of dopamine in their own financial lives must begin with a fundamental shift: moving from *outcome-driven* thinking to *purpose-driven* framing. The brain is far more likely to sustain effort when it believes the reward is meaningful. This means that simply setting revenue targets or growth metrics is unlikely to suffice unless those targets are clearly linked to something intrinsically valuable.

Purpose must therefore be translated into actionably personal terms. For some, this might mean associating financial growth with the ability to fund a particular cause, support a community, or leave a legacy. For others, it could mean achieving the freedom to work on what they love without compromise. When financial goals become extensions of personal values, they activate deeper motivational systems, making the pursuit itself more satisfying—even before success is achieved.

That said, purpose-driven individuals must also be cautious not to overload their sense of mission with excessive emotional weight. Paradoxically, if the stakes of a mission feel too existential, it can produce anxiety that inhibits motivation. The key is to find a balance: to frame goals in ways that are personally significant but also manageable and concrete. This aligns with research in goal-setting theory, which finds that specific, measurable, and attainable goals produce stronger motivation than abstract aspirations. When those goals are nested within a broader purpose, the motivational impact is magnified.

Another critical insight comes from the field of behavioural economics. The concept of *temporal discounting*—our tendency to devalue rewards the further they are in the future—can be countered by purpose. When the future reward carries emotional significance, it is perceived as more present and valuable, making it easier to delay gratification. This is essential for wealth-building, which often involves short-term sacrifices for long-term gains.

Purpose not only increases our capacity to wait—it makes the wait feel worthwhile.

This dynamic also underpins the success of vision-driven business models. Social enterprises and B Corps, for example, often see higher levels of employee engagement and customer loyalty—not because they offer higher salaries or cheaper products, but because their mission generates shared meaning. That shared meaning creates collective motivation, which in turn strengthens team cohesion, innovation, and perseverance. Internally, it means individuals are not just working for compensation, but for contribution. Externally, it creates a customer base willing to support a company not simply for what it sells, but for what it stands for.

One might ask, can dopamine-driven purpose be manufactured, or must it emerge organically? Neuroscience suggests that while deep purpose often arises from authentic experience, it can also be cultivated through narrative and reflection. When individuals reflect on past successes, connect daily tasks to larger goals, and visualise the long-term impact of their work, they increase dopamine production. This is why storytelling—both internal and external—is such a powerful motivational tool. It provides the brain with a coherent framework that links present effort to future significance.

For mission-driven entrepreneurs, this highlights the importance of periodically revisiting the "why" behind their work—not as a branding exercise, but as a neurological recharge. When motivation dips, the solution is not always more rest or external stimulation; sometimes, it is a deeper reconnection to meaning. Regular reflective practices—journaling, mentoring, strategic retreats—can help reactivate dormant motivation by bringing the emotional reward back into focus.

This understanding also reframes how we think about ambition. In traditional business culture, ambition is often equated with competitiveness or scale. But from a neuroscientific perspective, ambition grounded in purpose produces a qualitatively different motivational profile—one that is more sustainable, less volatile, and less susceptible to ego-driven distortions. Purpose-driven ambition is not about winning at all costs; it's about enduring with clarity.

Ultimately, the relationship between dopamine and purpose provides a powerful framework for rethinking motivation in the context of wealth creation. It suggests that the most effective way to build and sustain drive is not to chase more stimulation, but to deepen meaning. It reveals that financial success, when pursued as a means of fulfilling a purpose, can become neurologically self-reinforcing. And it affirms that in a world obsessed with outcomes, the true power lies in designing lives and businesses where the *pursuit itself* is rewarding.

To build wealth with purpose is to activate a higher-order motivation—one that is anchored not in fleeting rewards, but in enduring values. This is not only more ethical or more fulfilling; it is, as the science shows, more effective. Purpose doesn't just feel good. It works. And in the complex terrain of modern entrepreneurship, that may be the ultimate competitive advantage.

The Decision Fatigue Epidemic: Avoiding Burnout While Scaling Up

Entrepreneurship and leadership in the mission-driven economy are often portrayed as energising pursuits—full of vision, autonomy, and meaningful work. Yet the lived reality for many founders and purpose-led professionals is marked by a persistent undercurrent of cognitive exhaustion. Despite passion and clarity of purpose, they often find themselves overwhelmed, mentally depleted, and struggling to make decisions with the confidence and clarity they once possessed. The culprit is not laziness or incompetence, but a lesser-discussed phenomenon that drains even the most committed individuals: decision fatigue.

Decision fatigue refers to the psychological deterioration of decision-making quality after an extended period of decision activity. It is a subtle, cumulative drain on cognitive resources that, over time, impairs focus, narrows creativity, and increases susceptibility to impulsive or avoidant behaviours. While the condition affects everyone—from overextended parents to high-level executives—it is particularly acute for those scaling purpose-led ventures, where decisions often carry not only operational weight but also moral significance. When every choice feels high-stakes, mental depletion becomes a near-inevitable companion to ambition.

The science behind decision fatigue is robust and instructive. Groundbreaking research by social psychologist Roy Baumeister demonstrated that human willpower functions like a muscle: it can be exercised, but it also fatigues. In one of his most cited studies, participants asked to resist eating freshly baked cookies showed diminished performance on subsequent problem-solving tasks compared to those who were not presented with the same temptation. The implication is clear—every act of self-control or decision-making depletes a finite pool of mental energy, irrespective of the decision's magnitude.

Further research in neuroeconomics supports this view, revealing that the prefrontal cortex—responsible for rational thought, planning, and executive control—is especially sensitive to cumulative strain. When overloaded with decisions, this part of the brain shifts from deliberate processing to automatic, heuristic-driven responses. In a business context, this can lead to snap judgements, risk aversion, or paralysis, even in individuals known for their analytical rigour and strategic foresight.

One striking example of decision fatigue at work is seen in the criminal justice system. A 2011 study of Israeli parole board rulings found that judges were significantly more likely to grant parole at the beginning of the day or immediately after meal breaks. As the day progressed and cognitive fatigue set in, the default response shifted toward denial. These decisions, with serious consequences for people's lives, were influenced not by the facts of the case but by the decision-makers' depleted mental energy. If such bias can affect seasoned professionals in a structured environment, imagine its impact on entrepreneurs making hundreds of micro and macro decisions daily, often with limited information and time.

In mission-driven enterprises, the cognitive toll of decision-making is further compounded by the emotional weight of those decisions. Leaders are not simply asking, "What is the best financial move?" but "What aligns with our ethics, our impact goals, and our commitments to stakeholders?" These layers of moral and reputational complexity intensify the cognitive load and heighten the risk of burnout. It is not just the *number* of decisions that wears people down—it is the *significance* they assign to each one.

This raises an essential challenge: how can mission-led entrepreneurs scale without sacrificing clarity, conviction, or cognitive health?

One critical strategy is the systematic reduction of low-value decisions. Barack Obama famously wore the same style of suit every day during his presidency, explaining that he wanted to eliminate trivial choices so he could preserve his mental energy for more consequential matters. Similarly, Mark Zuckerberg adopted a uniform wardrobe and standardised meals to reduce decision friction. While these examples may seem extreme, they reflect a valuable principle: when routine choices are automated, cognitive bandwidth is freed for high-stakes thinking.

For entrepreneurs, this might mean establishing default settings in their calendar, automating aspects of financial tracking, or delegating authority to trusted team members with clear parameters. By building decision protocols and templates, they reduce the need to evaluate recurring issues from scratch. This is not about abdicating responsibility, but about conserving cognitive energy for creative and strategic problem-solving.

Another essential practice is the clarification of personal and organisational values. When values are explicitly articulated and embedded into decision-making frameworks, they serve as filters that streamline complexity. Consider Patagonia's approach under founder Yvon Chouinard: the company operates under the principle that environmental responsibility must be prioritised, even at a cost to short-term profit. This clarity enables faster, more confident decisions because it preempts endless deliberation about trade-offs. The company knows its north star, and so does everyone in it.

For smaller enterprises or solo entrepreneurs, a values audit can be a transformative exercise. By identifying core principles—such as transparency, community empowerment, or sustainability—and defining how they apply to business decisions, founders reduce ambiguity and increase decision speed without compromising mission integrity. When the "why" is pre-defined, the "how" becomes more manageable.

It is equally important to adopt a cadence of renewal. The brain's capacity for high-quality decision-making is replenished not through overwork, but through intentional rest. This is where the rhythm of the business must support the rhythm of the brain. Techniques such as decision batching—grouping similar decisions into defined time blocks—can help conserve energy. Setting aside non-negotiable time for recovery, whether through physical activity, unstructured thinking, or digital disconnection, is not indulgent; it is essential maintenance of executive function.

One instructive case study comes from Whitney Wolfe Herd, the founder and CEO of Bumble. Herd built a billion-dollar company by disrupting an industry while simultaneously navigating gendered scrutiny and operational complexity. She is known for instituting strong internal policies on mental wellness, including regular digital detoxes and structured team decision-making processes. By investing in cognitive and emotional sustainability—both hers and her team's—Herd has not only maintained her strategic focus but cultivated a resilient organisational culture.

Decision fatigue also underscores the importance of relational clarity. Entrepreneurs often expend enormous energy navigating interpersonal dynamics—whether with co-founders, clients, or collaborators. By setting clear boundaries, roles, and communication protocols early, they reduce ambiguity and interpersonal strain. A well-functioning team is not just a productivity booster; it is a buffer against the cognitive costs of carrying the entire decision burden alone.

There is also a psychological reframe that can ease the weight of leadership: not all decisions are equal, and not all demand perfection. The "maximiser" mindset—characterised by an obsessive quest for the optimal outcome—may appear virtuous, but research by Barry Schwartz has shown it often leads to regret, self-doubt, and delay. In contrast, "satisficers"—those who make good-enough decisions based on pre-set criteria—tend to experience less stress and more consistent progress. For mission-led individuals, the belief that every decision must reflect their deepest ideals can create a paralysing standard. Releasing that pressure and trusting in cumulative integrity, rather than perfection in every choice, is a hallmark of sustainable leadership.

Finally, purpose itself can act as a cognitive anchor. When leaders reconnect regularly with their mission—through storytelling, stakeholder feedback, or personal reflection—they fortify the motivational system that underpins resilience. Neuroscience tells us that purpose activates dopamine pathways associated with long-term effort. In practice, this means that decisions rooted in a meaningful vision are less likely to feel draining and more likely to feel energising, even under pressure.

The decision fatigue epidemic is real, but it is not insurmountable. With awareness, systems, and a renewed relationship to purpose, mission-driven individuals can scale their impact without depleting their energy or eroding their clarity. The goal is not to eliminate decision-making—it is to elevate it. To ensure that choices are guided by conviction, not exhaustion. And to build lives and businesses that grow not by burning through their cognitive resources, but by managing them with wisdom and care.

In a world that rewards speed, efficiency, and scale, the most radical act might be to slow down long enough to think clearly. Because the future of purpose-driven wealth depends not just on the decisions we make, but on the minds we bring to those decisions. Protecting that mental capital is not just good self-care—it is a strategic imperative.

Flow States and Focused Wealth Building

Productivity is often portrayed as a numbers game—an accumulation of hours worked, tasks completed, or metrics met. But this framing misses something essential: the quality of attention. In today's hyper-distracted world, where interruptions are constant and multitasking is mistaken for efficiency, the ability to direct full focus to a single, meaningful task has become rare—and immensely valuable. At the heart of high-performance success, particularly for entrepreneurs navigating complex challenges, lies a powerful but often underleveraged psychological phenomenon: the flow state.

First introduced by psychologist Mihaly Csikszentmihalyi in the 1970s, flow refers to a state of deep, immersive concentration in which individuals lose track of time and self-consciousness, fully absorbed in the task at hand. It is a mental zone where productivity and creativity converge, where effort feels almost effortless, and performance often peaks. Far from being a fringe or mystical experience, flow has been rigorously studied across domains—from elite sports to academic research, from musical performance to business innovation. It is now widely recognised as a foundational element of human excellence.

For entrepreneurs and mission-driven leaders, the relevance of flow is not just academic. In a landscape filled with decision fatigue, information overload, and competing demands, cultivating flow is a strategic necessity. It enables faster execution, deeper insight, and greater resilience. More importantly, it aligns perfectly with the ethos of purpose-driven wealth building—because flow is most easily achieved when one is engaged in meaningful, self-directed work that presents just the right level of challenge.

Csikszentmihalyi's research revealed that flow emerges when three key conditions are met: a clear goal, immediate feedback, and a balance between skill level and task difficulty. When the challenge exceeds one's skills, anxiety ensues. When skills exceed the challenge, boredom sets in. But when the two are in harmony, the brain enters a state of focused efficiency marked by heightened dopamine activity, reduced activity in the default mode network (which is associated with self-referential thoughts), and increased synchronisation between cognitive and motor regions. This neurophysiological cocktail creates not only optimal performance but deep satisfaction.

In the context of entrepreneurship, this has profound implications. Start-up founders, solopreneurs, and scale-stage executives are routinely pulled in multiple directions. Strategy, operations, product development, marketing, finance—the list of responsibilities is endless. The fragmentation of attention that results can easily derail both effectiveness and mental well-being. Flow offers a remedy, not by reducing complexity, but by enabling selective immersion.

Take, for example, the case of Jack Dorsey, who at one point was simultaneously CEO of both Twitter and Square. To maintain performance across two demanding companies, Dorsey famously structured his week into themed days—Mondays for management, Tuesdays for product, and so on. This compartmentalisation was more than just a time-management hack; it was a way to protect blocks of uninterrupted focus, thereby increasing the likelihood of entering flow. Rather than constantly shifting between unrelated tasks, he designed his schedule around depth over breadth.

Similarly, successful creators like Cal Newport, author of *Deep Work*, have popularised the idea that uninterrupted focus is now a competitive advantage. Newport's thesis, grounded in cognitive science, asserts that knowledge workers who cultivate the ability to concentrate deeply on cognitively demanding tasks will outpace their distracted peers. This is particularly true for entrepreneurs who are not just executing routines but solving novel problems—developing products, crafting narratives, building systems. These are the very tasks most conducive to flow, but they are also the most vulnerable to distraction.

Flow, when consistently accessed, becomes a flywheel. It accelerates learning, improves decision-making, and enhances emotional resilience. This is not merely theoretical. Research published in *The Journal of Positive Psychology* shows that individuals who regularly experience flow report higher levels of overall well-being, greater life satisfaction, and reduced anxiety. For entrepreneurs, this means that flow is not just a productivity tool—it's a psychological asset that can buffer against burnout and enhance long-term performance.

But while the science of flow is well-established, the practice of cultivating it requires deliberate action. One critical step is environmental design. Flow flourishes in distraction-free zones. This means turning off notifications, minimising open tabs, and designing physical or digital spaces that cue focus. Entrepreneur and investor Naval Ravikant describes working in "low-stimulation environments" as a key driver of clarity and creativity. His approach echoes a broader trend among high-performing individuals: a conscious rejection of noise in favour of depth.

Another vital factor is goal structuring. Flow requires clarity. Vague tasks such as "work on strategy" or "grow the business" do not offer the specificity needed to trigger deep focus. By contrast, tasks like "outline the next three months of the product roadmap" or "craft investor pitch for upcoming funding round" offer defined endpoints and measurable progress. This clarity, combined with real-time feedback—whether through external metrics or internal cues—creates the conditions for flow to emerge.

There's also an emotional dimension to flow that resonates deeply with purpose-driven individuals. Csikszentmihalyi found that flow is not associated with passive pleasure but with *active engagement.* People in flow are often pushing their limits, stretching their abilities, and immersing themselves in service of something larger than themselves. For entrepreneurs working toward a meaningful mission, this alignment between challenge, skill, and purpose is particularly potent. It transforms work from obligation into vocation—from something one *has* to do into something one *wants* to master.

A notable example is Scott Harrison, founder of charity: water. Building a non-profit from scratch into one of the most trusted and transparent organisations in the philanthropic sector required not only vision but sustained focus. Harrison often recounts long, focused stretches of creative work—designing campaigns, writing appeals, structuring partnerships—during which he lost all sense of time. His flow was fuelled not by the promise of personal gain, but by the conviction that his work was solving a life-threatening problem. The emotional resonance of the mission enhanced his cognitive performance.

Entrepreneurs who build around their flow zones—whether in writing, coding, selling, or strategising—tend to scale more effectively because they are operating in their zone of highest leverage. They are not wasting energy battling distractions or second-guessing themselves. They are building momentum. And momentum, in entrepreneurship, often matters more than perfection.

However, the cultivation of flow is not without its challenges. The modern work environment is increasingly hostile to depth. Slack messages, email pings, and the culture of instant response fragment attention and punish patience. Mission-driven entrepreneurs must therefore treat flow not as an occasional luxury, but as a non-negotiable discipline. Just as physical training requires commitment and consistency, so does training the mind to enter and sustain flow.

This is where rituals can be useful. Many creatives and founders swear by pre-flow routines—brief walks, meditative breathing, music, or specific lighting conditions—that signal to the brain it's time to engage. These rituals, over time, become anchors, helping the brain shift from surface-level awareness into deep concentration more readily.

The benefits extend beyond individual performance. Teams that are structured around flow principles—minimal meetings, asynchronous communication, clear task ownership—tend to be more productive and more satisfied. They experience fewer conflicts, less burnout, and higher retention. Flow, when scaled across a culture, becomes a competitive differentiator. It creates a rhythm of execution that feels energising rather than depleting.

Ultimately, focused wealth building is not about working longer hours or saying yes to every opportunity. It is about identifying where you produce the highest value with the least resistance and designing your life and business to amplify that. Flow is the gateway to that state. It enables you to work not harder, but deeper. And when that depth is aligned with purpose, the outcomes—financial and emotional—are not only sustainable, they are transformative.

In a society that often equates success with speed, reclaiming the power of focused attention is a radical act. It is a reminder that excellence does not emerge from noise or haste, but from concentrated engagement with what matters most. Flow is not a buzzword or a passing trend. It is a scientifically grounded, human-centred approach to creating, scaling, and sustaining wealth with intention. For entrepreneurs seeking not just to grow, but to thrive with purpose, flow is not a side benefit—it is the engine.

Scarcity vs. Abundance Mindset: Why Mission-Driven People Struggle with Money

It is a paradox that confounds even the most socially conscious entrepreneurs: the same individuals who lead with vision, serve with empathy, and pour their energies into addressing the world's most pressing issues often find themselves entangled in financial struggle or discomfort. These are not people lacking in discipline, intelligence, or ambition. They are driven by purpose, yet disproportionately hesitant to pursue—or even accept—financial success. The source of this tension is not logistical but psychological. At its core lies a subtle yet deeply entrenched belief system: the scarcity mindset.

Coined by Stephen Covey and later expanded by researchers such as Dr Carol Dweck and Dr Sendhil Mullainathan, the scarcity mindset is characterised by a pervasive focus on limitations—of time, money, resources, and opportunities. It leads individuals to make decisions based on fear, constraint, and perceived lack. While anyone can fall into this pattern, purpose-led professionals are particularly susceptible because of their relationship with money: one that is often shaped by moral ambivalence, inherited beliefs, or unconscious loyalty to an anti-capitalist ethos.

Many mission-driven entrepreneurs unconsciously carry the notion that wealth and virtue exist in a zero-sum equation—that profit, by definition, compromises purpose. This belief is often rooted in formative experiences. Some were raised in environments where financial ambition was viewed as selfish or superficial. Others internalised narratives that conflated material success with greed or injustice. These narratives, while often socially reinforced, create a cognitive dissonance: the more one seeks to earn, the more one fears betraying their ethical identity.

This mindset doesn't merely inhibit wealth accumulation; it distorts the entire decision-making process. Entrepreneurs operating from scarcity often undercharge for their services, overextend themselves with unpaid labour, and hesitate to invest in growth. They may avoid strategic risk, reject well-deserved recognition, or sabotage opportunities for fear of appearing "too commercial." The result is a business that may appear noble on the surface but is structurally unsustainable—draining the founder's energy while failing to scale the mission they care about.

In contrast, the abundance mindset represents a fundamentally different orientation. It assumes that resources—financial, emotional, intellectual—are not fixed but expansive. Abundance thinking enables entrepreneurs to recognise money as a tool, not a test of character. It reframes wealth creation as a form of resource stewardship: the more financially resourced one is, the more they can invest in people, innovation, and systemic change. This shift does not require abandoning ethics or altruism; it requires integrating them into a more empowered relationship with value and exchange.

A striking example of this transformation can be seen in the story of Danielle LaPorte, a writer and entrepreneur who began her career in the non-profit world and initially struggled with the idea of monetising her work. For years, LaPorte underpriced her services and avoided conventional marketing, fearing that financial ambition would dilute her spiritual message. Eventually, she recognised that her discomfort with money was limiting not only her own potential but her ability to serve her audience at scale. By reframing her approach—seeing money as an amplifier of impact rather than a corrupting force—she built a thriving business while remaining uncompromising in her values.

This kind of mindset shift is not just anecdotal—it is supported by a growing body of psychological research. Dr Carol Dweck's concept of the "growth mindset," though initially focused on learning and intelligence, has profound implications for financial behaviour. Individuals with a growth mindset view challenges as opportunities and believe their abilities can evolve. Applied to money, this means seeing financial skill as learnable, not innate, and wealth as buildable, not bestowed. It encourages experimentation, resilience, and openness—all critical traits for entrepreneurs navigating uncertainty.

Neuroscience further validates the power of abundance thinking. Studies on neuroplasticity reveal that thought patterns can be reshaped through consistent practice and reframing. When individuals consciously focus on possibility rather than limitation, they begin to alter the brain's default mode network—responsible for internal dialogue and self-perception. This rewiring reduces anxiety, increases cognitive flexibility, and enhances problem-solving, making individuals more capable of identifying and seizing financial opportunities aligned with their mission.

One of the most damaging features of the scarcity mindset is the false binary it imposes between service and sustainability. It suggests that doing meaningful work necessitates personal sacrifice, and that seeking compensation for one's talents is somehow ethically suspect. This belief is particularly entrenched in social enterprise and non-profit sectors, where phrases like "lean" or "scrappy" are often worn as badges of honour. But austerity is not a moral virtue; it is a structural vulnerability. When organisations and their leaders are under-resourced, their capacity to innovate, retain talent, and deliver long-term value is compromised.

The shift to abundance requires not only internal reframing but also external modelling. When purpose-driven entrepreneurs see peers who have built profitable, value-aligned ventures, it helps dismantle the subconscious link between money and moral compromise. Consider the case of Tensie Whelan, former president of the Rainforest Alliance and now a professor at NYU Stern. Her leadership exemplified how rigorous financial strategy and mission integrity can coexist. Under her tenure, the organisation significantly expanded its global reach and revenue while maintaining its ecological and social commitments. Her work has since inspired a new generation of sustainability professionals to view profit not as an enemy of impact, but as a partner in it.

Practical strategies for fostering an abundance mindset often begin with language. The way entrepreneurs talk about money—internally and externally—shapes their behaviour. Replacing phrases like "I can't afford that" with "How might I fund that?" opens up neural pathways for creativity. Shifting from "What will people think if I charge this much?" to "What is the value I am providing?" reframes pricing from self-worth to service. These micro-adjustments, repeated over time, recalibrate one's entire orientation toward money.

Another lever is visibility. Many purpose-driven individuals fear visibility not because they lack confidence in their work, but because they associate visibility with ego or exposure. Yet staying invisible is often the fastest path to burnout and irrelevance. Financial sustainability requires a willingness to be seen, to share the story of one's work, and to invite others into it—through clients, partnerships, or investment. Visibility, when rooted in service, becomes not self-promotion but mission amplification.

Moreover, embracing abundance does not mean denying constraints. It means responding to them with creativity rather than defeat. When the COVID-19 pandemic disrupted industries, many mission-led entrepreneurs pivoted with remarkable agility—not because they were exempt from limitation, but because they were practiced in resourcefulness. Those with an abundance mindset asked better questions: "What new needs are emerging? How can we repurpose our skills? Where are the underutilised assets?" These questions reflect a belief that even in crisis, value can be created.

Perhaps the most important shift is from scarcity to sufficiency. Abundance is not about endless accumulation; it's about enoughness. It's about recognising that wealth is not merely financial but relational, emotional, and intellectual. When mission-driven entrepreneurs begin to appreciate the full spectrum of their capital—not just what's in the bank but what's in their ideas, communities, and networks—they operate from a place of empowerment rather than deprivation. From this place, financial growth becomes a reflection of alignment, not compromise.

Scarcity thinking is pervasive, but it is not immutable. With reflection, support, and deliberate practice, entrepreneurs can rewire their relationship with money—transforming it from a source of stress or shame into a tool for impact and integrity. The invitation is not to abandon ideals but to expand them—to build ventures where purpose and prosperity not only coexist but reinforce one another.

Because when those committed to changing the world also learn to embrace wealth, they don't just survive. They scale. And the world doesn't need fewer mission-driven entrepreneurs—it needs more of them who are resourced, resilient, and ready to lead.

Interactive Exercise: Your Money Mission Brainstorm

For mission-driven individuals, financial goal-setting can often feel like stepping into a paradox. On one hand, there's the desire for economic stability, freedom, and even abundance. On the other, a persistent internal tug: a discomfort with traditional financial ambition, a fear of being perceived as overly commercial, or a suspicion that monetary goals might dilute the purity of purpose. These tensions are not merely philosophical—they are deeply psychological and, unless consciously addressed, can create confusion, inaction, and even sabotage.

To break through this impasse, we must reframe the way financial goals are conceived—not as isolated figures on a spreadsheet, but as expressions of personal values and mission. This is the essence of the *Money Mission Brainstorm*, a structured reflective practice designed to bring clarity, coherence, and emotional alignment to the financial dimensions of a purposeful life or venture. When done thoughtfully, this exercise doesn't just yield financial targets.

It generates insight into what truly matters, what drives your ambition, and what kind of legacy you want to leave.

At its core, this exercise invites you to ask a different kind of question. Not, "How much do I want to earn?" but "What does my ideal financial life *enable* me to do?" This shift is subtle but profound. It transforms money from a static end goal into a dynamic enabler of mission-aligned action. It also surfaces subconscious beliefs—about sufficiency, worthiness, and fear—that often remain hidden beneath layers of strategic planning.

To begin, it's helpful to reflect on a few foundational concepts drawn from psychology and behavioural economics. The first is the principle of *goal congruence*. Research by Locke and Latham, pioneers in the field of goal-setting theory, shows that goals are most motivating when they are internally consistent with a person's values and identity. Goals that are externally imposed or socially conditioned tend to create resistance or burnout. In contrast, congruent goals generate a state of what self-determination theory refers to as "autonomous motivation"—where action flows from a deep sense of ownership and alignment. In practice, this means your financial targets should feel like a natural extension of your broader mission—not arbitrary numbers dictated by industry standards or peer comparisons.

Consider the example of Binta Niambi Brown, a corporate attorney turned social entrepreneur. After a successful legal career, Brown founded Fermata Entertainment, a music company designed to give underrepresented artists greater ownership and agency. Her financial goals were shaped not by the music industry's obsession with celebrity or scale, but by a desire to model ethical business practices in creative economies. Brown's revenue models were deliberately structured to reflect her values—prioritising transparency, fair compensation, and cultural equity. Her financial decisions were never divorced from her mission; they were a vehicle for it.

This kind of thinking is at the heart of the Money Mission Brainstorm. It involves surfacing and articulating not just what you want to earn, but *why* you want to earn it—and what structures, boundaries, and values must be in place for that income to feel meaningful and ethical. It also requires honesty about constraints. What trade-offs are you unwilling to make? What kinds of clients or industries would compromise your mission, even if they offered higher financial return? These reflections are not just about idealism. They are about creating a durable and emotionally sustainable framework for financial growth.

Neuroscience adds another layer of insight here. When goals are tied to emotionally salient outcomes, they activate the brain's dopaminergic reward system, making it more likely that we will stay motivated through long-term effort. This explains why financial goals that feel generic—like "earn six figures" or "double revenue"—often fail to inspire action. The brain does not respond to abstraction. It responds to *meaning*. When money is clearly linked to something emotionally resonant—such as supporting a community, funding a creative project, or achieving time freedom—the motivational circuits light up, and the pursuit becomes energised rather than burdensome.

A useful way to activate this process is through visualisation. Imagine your ideal financial year—not just in terms of income, but in terms of how that income is used, what it supports, and how it feels. Where does the money go? What does your daily life look like? What decisions do you no longer have to make? This kind of narrative thinking engages both hemispheres of the brain, linking logic with emotion, and helping to create a vivid cognitive map of your money mission.

One entrepreneur who leveraged this kind of exercise is Jessamyn Stanley, founder of The Underbelly, a wellness platform designed to make yoga more inclusive. Stanley, whose brand challenges mainstream ideals of body image, built her financial strategy around access, representation, and equity. Her income goals were calibrated not around maximising profit, but around creating a sustainable infrastructure that would allow her to scale her message without compromising its integrity. Through strategic partnerships, content licensing, and membership models, Stanley's revenue structure now funds a broader mission of cultural transformation—while providing personal financial security.

The Money Mission Brainstorm also serves a diagnostic function. It reveals where old stories about money may be interfering with current goals. Many mission-led individuals carry inherited beliefs—whether from family, culture, or past experiences—that money is dangerous, morally suspect, or corrupting. These narratives often operate unconsciously, creating friction between what people *say* they want financially and what they are willing to pursue. Surfacing these beliefs and interrogating their origins can free up enormous psychological energy. When people replace shame with agency, scarcity with strategy, their financial behaviour changes—often dramatically.

For example, consider the experience of a purpose-driven coach who consistently struggled to charge sustainable rates despite delivering exceptional value. Through guided reflection, she recognised that she had internalised a belief that helping others should come without cost. This belief, though noble in intent, was undermining her business viability and causing personal burnout. By reframing her pricing as a reflection of energy exchange—not just financial transaction—she was able to raise her rates, attract more committed clients, and create new offerings that better served both her mission and her bank account.

Ultimately, the Money Mission Brainstorm is not a static worksheet. It is a dynamic process of inquiry, alignment, and design. It asks not just what you want to earn, but who you are becoming in the process. It requires that you integrate the emotional, ethical, and strategic dimensions of wealth in a way that reflects your unique voice and values. It challenges the false dichotomy between purpose and profit—and offers a structured way to hold both with integrity.

As a practical application, this exercise works best when returned to periodically—at the start of a new year, a business cycle, or after a significant transition. Goals will shift as your understanding of purpose evolves. But the core insight remains constant: when money is placed in the service of meaning, it becomes a tool for liberation rather than limitation. And when financial strategy is rooted in personal truth, it becomes not just effective—but deeply fulfilling.

In a culture that too often pits moral clarity against financial competence, the Money Mission Brainstorm offers a third path: one of thoughtful integration. It reminds us that money is neither sacred nor profane. It is a mirror. And when we look into it with courage and clarity, what we often find is not greed or guilt—but a roadmap to a life more deeply aligned with who we really are and what we most want to give.

Chapter 3
Monetising Mission Without Selling Out

Few tensions gnaw more persistently at the conscience of purpose-driven entrepreneurs than the dread of betraying their values in pursuit of profit. It's the murmur behind closed doors during pricing negotiations, the hesitation before launching a campaign, the quiet doubt that arises when envisioning scale: "If I push too hard for revenue, do I risk losing the soul of what I've built?" This concern is far from unfounded. It's rooted in a cultural narrative that has long set purpose and profit at odds—as though one must be noble and the other, inherently tainted. But this dichotomy, while seductive in its simplicity, is false. Worse, it's a barrier. Because meaningful impact, if it is to last, must be underpinned by financial stability. Monetisation, done ethically and with strategic clarity, isn't the enemy of mission—it's its most faithful ally.

So, we arrive at the central provocation of this chapter: How does one build genuine income without watering down their ideals? The answer lies not in compromise, but in reimagining how integrity functions within the mechanics of business. Here, we'll delve into the mental shifts, operational decisions, and behavioural choices that distinguish enduring, financially robust mission-led ventures from the kind of heartfelt side projects that, while noble, rarely sustain themselves. This isn't a defence of profit—it's an invitation to elevate what a values-driven business can be. One where authenticity isn't just preserved but leveraged, not as an afterthought but as the sharpest edge in a crowded marketplace.

Let's start by confronting a hard, uncomfortable truth: passion, on its own, is a terrible business plan. Many purpose-led projects don't falter due to lack of commitment or inspiration. They fail because they never got the commercial structure right. There's a persistent myth—especially in spaces that traffic in idealism—that sheer conviction is enough to carry a venture. But a dream, no matter how noble, needs scaffolding. It needs revenue pathways, operational clarity, and a grasp of market dynamics. Too often, founders mistake applause for demand, or confuse a large social following with meaningful sales. What's frequently missing isn't enthusiasm—it's a monetisation strategy that links mission to repeatable value.

This doesn't mean watering things down. On the contrary, it means refining the mission into something tangible—something others will pay for, not because they're being charitable, but because they genuinely see the value. Purpose shouldn't be a reason to play small; it should be the impetus to scale, smartly and with care.

Among the most potent assets in this recalibration is authenticity. In a business landscape increasingly saturated with curated messaging and slick branding, consumers are drawn to what feels real. They want congruence between what a brand says and what it does. When there's harmony between message and model, trust emerges—and in today's economy, trust may well be the most powerful driver of conversion.

Consumer psychology backs this up. A 2020 paper in the *Journal of Consumer Research* found that buyers who perceive a brand as mission-driven display greater loyalty and advocacy—even when alternatives are cheaper or more convenient. This isn't a soft benefit. It's a strategic differentiator. When people believe in your purpose and see it woven into the fabric of your operations, they don't just buy from you—they build with you.

Take Everlane, the fashion label that gained traction not by out-styling its competitors, but by blowing the doors off the black box of pricing. With its "radical transparency" approach, Everlane revealed production costs and margins—something most brands would consider unthinkable. And it worked. Not because the clothes were earth-shatteringly unique, but because the brand's integrity was visible. The trust it cultivated became a moat, a magnet. Their transparency wasn't just ethical; it was strategic.

But authenticity alone won't carry a business across the finish line. One of the more insidious traps awaiting mission-led founders is the pricing paradox: the deeply ingrained belief that doing good should come with a financial discount. This reflex—to charge less, to give away services, to downplay one's value—is often wrapped in virtue, but it's costly. Left unchecked, it produces a cycle of under-resourcing, overworking, and underdelivering, all of which ultimately cap the business's reach and the founder's wellbeing.

There's a necessary mindset shift here. Purpose does not license martyrdom. In fact, it demands a pricing model that reflects not just the cost of production or hours invested, but the true value of delivering impact sustainably. Ethical pricing is not about bending over backwards for affordability—it's about clarity, alignment, and longevity. It's about asking: what does it cost to keep this mission alive and thriving?

This is particularly salient in service-based ventures, where the product is often invisible—expertise, time, presence, emotional labour. When purpose-led coaches, consultants, or educators undercharge from fear or misplaced humility, they set in motion a pattern that can be hard to break. Pricing fairly isn't greed—it's responsibility. It signals seriousness, sustains energy, and supports scale.

And scale, for many founders, is where the fear creeps back in. There's a sense that growing too big too fast might attract the wrong investors, compromise values, or invite structures that prioritise efficiency over ethics. These concerns aren't paranoid; they're legitimate. But they aren't destiny. It is entirely possible to grow with integrity—if the systems that support the business are built from the beginning to uphold, rather than erode, its mission.

There are living examples of this. Warby Parker, the eyewear company that popularised the "buy a pair, give a pair" model, scaled dramatically while keeping its values front and centre. Mission wasn't tacked on—it was baked in. It shaped hiring, informed design, and helped direct expansion. Their model didn't survive growth; it powered it.

Likewise, consider Tiffany Aliche, better known as The Budgetnista. She began with a humble blog aimed at improving financial literacy for women of colour. No fancy backers, no glossy PR campaigns—just real, relevant content. Over time, she built a multi-million-pound enterprise, complete with bestselling books, partnerships, and educational platforms. Her secret? Relentless focus on accessibility without compromising her business model. She created tiered offerings—free for those who needed it, paid for those who could afford it. Everyone was served, and no one was short-changed.

These are not exceptions. They're a glimpse of what's possible when profit and purpose are designed to co-exist—not in uneasy truce, but in genuine collaboration. The real challenge lies in the architecture. It's not enough to declare values; they have to be operationalised—baked into pricing, product development, recruitment, and funding decisions.

This chapter will explore how to do exactly that: how to turn purpose into value, how to write copy that resonates without resorting to clichés, how to price with confidence and build with intention. There's also a real-world profile of a nonprofit founder who grew her mission into a $10 million impact enterprise without ever compromising her ethics. Her journey rewrites the rules of what success can look like.

Ultimately, monetising purpose without selling out requires a different lens. It means recognising that money isn't a contaminant, but a conduit. It doesn't need to threaten your integrity—it can express it. When handled with discernment, monetisation is not a deflection from purpose; it is the means by which that purpose travels further, louder, and with greater force. Because in a world where noise is cheap and trust is scarce, the businesses that last aren't the ones that follow every trend or chase every dollar. They're the ones that know who they are, charge accordingly, and grow from that place—steadfast, rooted, and unapologetically clear.

From Passion to Profit: The Missing Link

For many aspiring entrepreneurs, the conventional wisdom is clear: follow your passion, and success will follow. The idea is seductively simple—do what you love, and the money will somehow take care of itself. It is a mantra echoed in motivational speeches, Instagram quotes, and countless business self-help books. Yet when scrutinised through the lens of lived entrepreneurial experience, this narrative begins to fracture. While passion is undeniably powerful as a source of motivation, it is rarely sufficient to build a sustainable, scalable business. In truth, most passion projects fail not for lack of heart, but for lack of structure. The missing link is not enthusiasm, but a sound, adaptive, and strategically aligned business model.

Passion, by its nature, is emotive. It ignites creativity, fuels persistence, and brings a sense of personal meaning to work. However, it is also inherently subjective and often blind to market reality. What excites you may not resonate with others. What feels urgent or valuable to you may not solve a clearly defined problem that others are willing to pay for. In economic terms, passion alone does not create demand. To convert passion into profit, entrepreneurs must bridge the gap between personal inspiration and market relevance.

This requires a reframing of how passion is positioned within the business-building process. Rather than being the end itself, passion should be understood as the fuel—necessary, but not sufficient. The engine is strategy: product-market fit, pricing, delivery, differentiation, and scalability. Without these elements, passion becomes a liability—leading to overcommitment, underpricing, and burnout.

One of the most common pitfalls is confusing audience validation with customer conversion. A creator may receive praise, social media engagement, or even viral success for their content or product, only to find that this visibility does not translate into actual revenue. The problem often lies in the absence of a clear value proposition and monetisation pathway. Likes are not transactions, and attention is not loyalty. To make the leap to profit, entrepreneurs must identify what specific problem their product or service solves, for whom, and why those individuals would choose to pay for it.

A case in point is the experience of Kristen Ley, founder of Thimblepress, a creative stationery and lifestyle company that began as a side project fuelled by her love of art and design. Ley's passion was unmistakable, and her handcrafted products quickly gained a following on platforms like Etsy. But initial growth plateaued when she realised that enthusiasm alone couldn't scale the business. She began analysing purchasing data, streamlining her product lines, and building partnerships with major retailers. By integrating structure into her passion, she transformed Thimblepress from a personal outlet into a nationally recognised brand. Her success did not stem from abandoning her creative roots, but from learning to channel them through a commercial lens.

This transformation—from passion to profitability—requires a shift from internal focus to external orientation. Passion asks, "What do I love to create?" Strategy asks, "What does the market value?" The sweet spot lies in the overlap: a product or service that reflects your values and creativity while meeting a tangible need in a way that is differentiated, desirable, and deliverable at scale.

This distinction is particularly important for mission-led entrepreneurs, who often assume that the nobility of their cause guarantees support. But a mission, however meaningful, must be translated into outcomes that clients or customers can clearly understand and access. As marketing strategist Donald Miller points out, people don't buy the best products or services; they buy the ones they understand the fastest. Mission-driven founders must learn to articulate their impact in language that resonates with their audience's needs—not just their ideals.

The financial model is another crucial piece of the equation. Many passion projects remain financially fragile because their creators are uncomfortable engaging with pricing, margin, or profitability. They view money as a by-product, an afterthought, or even a contaminant of their creative or ethical work. But purpose and profit are not mutually exclusive. In fact, when approached with integrity, pricing becomes a mechanism for sustainability. Charging appropriately allows entrepreneurs to reinvest in quality, expand access, pay fair wages, and increase their impact over time. Underpricing, by contrast, often leads to overextension, resentment, and compromised quality.

The pricing model should not be determined by guilt, fear, or peer comparison, but by a clear understanding of value and viability. Entrepreneurs need to account for their time, materials, intellectual capital, and emotional labour—particularly in service-based fields where these inputs are easily underestimated. Transparent, fair pricing is not exploitative. It is the foundation of a stable business that can consistently deliver value without sacrificing the well-being of its creator.

There is also a structural aspect to moving from passion to profit that is frequently overlooked: the creation of systems. Passion projects are often highly personalised, with the founder acting as the sole creator, marketer, and operator. This makes the business emotionally rewarding but operationally fragile. Without replicable systems for delivery, customer acquisition, and client onboarding, growth becomes a trap rather than an opportunity. Every new sale adds to the founder's workload instead of increasing capacity or freedom.

The solution is to move from craft to company—without losing the essence of the original passion. This does not mean abandoning the unique personal touch that defines many small businesses. It means designing backend processes, automating repetitive tasks, and creating documentation so that the business can function without constant reinvention. It means hiring not just out of desperation, but with an eye toward culture fit and role clarity. Founders who systematise early can maintain the soul of their work while expanding its reach.

The evolution from passion to profit is not about dilution; it is about translation. It is the process of taking something meaningful and making it accessible, repeatable, and sustainable. It is about matching vision with viability, art with architecture. And perhaps most critically, it is about cultivating the mindset that financial success does not negate purpose—it enables it.

Take the example of Jessica Jackley, co-founder of Kiva, the microlending platform that has facilitated over $1.5 billion in loans to underserved entrepreneurs worldwide. Jackley's passion for economic justice was the catalyst, but her impact was made possible by her willingness to engage rigorously with business modelling, financial risk, and platform design. Kiva's success didn't come from idealism alone; it came from operational excellence rooted in purpose.

What this illustrates is a broader principle: purpose-driven entrepreneurs must become fluent in both the language of meaning and the mechanics of business. They must know how to speak to the heart and build for scale. Passion lights the fire, but profit keeps it burning.

To succeed in today's economy, it is no longer enough to love what you do. You must also build a model that sustains what you love—economically, operationally, and psychologically. You must be willing to test, adapt, and evolve—not to chase trends, but to refine your value in the eyes of those you seek to serve. Only then can passion become more than a feeling. Only then can it become a force. A force not just for personal fulfilment, but for meaningful, measurable, and scalable impact.

Authenticity Sells: The Psychology of Trust and Connection

In a marketplace saturated with choice and fuelled by scepticism, one quality increasingly separates brands that thrive from those that flounder: authenticity. Amid flashy marketing campaigns, influencer endorsements, and algorithm-driven advertising, consumers are tuning their attention toward brands that feel real—transparent, principled, and emotionally resonant. This is not a passing trend or a millennial quirk. It is a reflection of deep-seated psychological drivers that shape how people perceive value, assess trustworthiness, and make purchasing decisions.

The growing demand for authenticity is not merely cultural—it is cognitive. Research in behavioural economics and psychology consistently shows that trust is a primary determinant of buying behaviour. When people sense inconsistency, exaggeration, or insincerity, their cognitive defences go up. The brain, hardwired to detect incongruity as a threat, instinctively withdraws. Conversely, when a brand consistently aligns its words with its actions, shares its imperfections as well as its triumphs, and communicates in a human voice, it creates what psychologists call cognitive coherence—a sense that "this feels right." That sense of rightness, while often subconscious, significantly impacts consumer behaviour.

This psychological dynamic is particularly relevant to mission-based businesses. Brands built around purpose have a unique advantage in cultivating trust because they offer more than a transaction; they offer a worldview. When consumers see that a business is animated by values that align with their own, the relationship transcends product utility and becomes emotionally meaningful. They are not just buying a coffee—they are supporting fair trade. They are not just purchasing cosmetics—they are investing in cruelty-free production. These deeper connections foster loyalty, advocacy, and resilience in the face of competition.

A case in point is Patagonia, a company frequently cited not just for its environmental ethos but for how transparently and consistently it lives those values. From repairing customers' old jackets rather than selling them new ones, to suing the Trump administration over public land protection, Patagonia's brand is not manufactured—it is demonstrated. The company's annual revenue has exceeded a billion dollars not by pursuing growth at any cost, but by anchoring every decision to a well-communicated mission. The result is not only a robust business, but one that enjoys deep consumer devotion and cultural capital disproportionate to its size.

What makes this kind of brand loyalty so powerful is that it is built on what researchers call affective trust—trust that is rooted not just in competence, but in emotional alignment. Consumers are increasingly aware that businesses are not just economic actors but cultural agents. When a brand's values feel authentic, consumers feel seen, affirmed, and proud to be associated with it. This emotional resonance is especially important in the post-pandemic economy, where trust in institutions—including corporations—has been severely eroded.

Yet authenticity cannot be faked. Attempts to simulate it—through performative social campaigns, hollow sustainability pledges, or opportunistic value signalling—tend to backfire. Savvy consumers now expect transparency to be verifiable. They seek evidence, not just rhetoric. This shift has put pressure on companies to align their internal practices with their external messaging. It has also created an opportunity for smaller, more agile mission-based brands to outperform larger competitors who struggle to adapt their legacy systems to these new expectations.

The psychology of connection extends beyond branding to every touchpoint of the customer experience. Authenticity is communicated not just in mission statements but in tone of voice, customer service interactions, packaging, website design, and post-sale engagement. When these elements are thoughtfully aligned, they create a sense of integrity—a brand personality that feels coherent and trustworthy. When they are disjointed or formulaic, trust erodes quickly, regardless of the product's objective quality.

Consider the success of Who Gives A Crap, an eco-friendly toilet paper company that donates 50% of its profits to building sanitation infrastructure in developing countries. From the irreverent tone of its packaging to the transparency of its impact reports, the brand communicates a sense of personality and purpose that immediately differentiates it from traditional players. The company's humour does not undermine its seriousness—it humanises its mission, making it approachable and compelling. By aligning its communication style with its values, it fosters a sense of trust that has translated into explosive growth, even in a commoditised market.

This alignment is crucial because authenticity is not a static trait; it is a perception created through consistency over time. Mission-based businesses must understand that every action—from supplier selection to crisis response—either reinforces or undermines that perception. When decisions are guided by clear principles, communicated transparently, and delivered with empathy, authenticity is reinforced. When they are made expediently, opaquely, or inconsistently, trust erodes—and with it, customer loyalty.

Another dimension of authenticity lies in the founder's story. In a media landscape where audiences crave realness, the personal narrative of a company's creator can serve as a powerful trust-building asset. When shared with humility and purpose, a founder's background can become a touchstone for authenticity. Take the example of Sara Blakely, founder of Spanx, who often recounts how she started the company with $5,000 in savings and no experience in fashion. Her candid, self-deprecating storytelling has not only humanised the brand but inspired a global customer base who sees her success as both relatable and aspirational.

However, it is important to note that authenticity does not mean overexposure. The goal is not to broadcast every detail of a company's internal workings or every facet of a founder's personal life. It is to tell the truth selectively, but sincerely—to choose stories, facts, and messages that reflect the company's values and speak meaningfully to its audience. Authenticity is as much about restraint as it is about disclosure. It is about sharing enough to be real, but not so much that the message becomes muddled or self-indulgent.

There is also a compelling business case for this approach. Studies conducted by the Harvard Business Review and Edelman Trust Barometer have consistently shown that trust-based branding improves key performance indicators across the board—from conversion rates to customer retention to employee engagement. Employees, too, are more likely to stay loyal and perform at a higher level when they believe the company's mission is authentic and lived internally. In an era of conscious capitalism, authenticity is no longer a soft skill; it is a hard advantage.

Mission-driven businesses must therefore treat authenticity not as an optional add-on, but as an operating principle. This involves embedding values into decision-making frameworks, training teams to communicate with integrity, and creating feedback loops that allow customers to see how their voices are being heard and their values reflected. It means being willing to admit mistakes publicly, to evolve openly, and to demonstrate that mission is not a slogan but a standard.

As more consumers begin to vote with their wallets—seeking not just utility but alignment—brands that cultivate authentic connection will increasingly outperform those that chase attention with gimmicks. Trust is not built by noise, but by nuance. By showing up consistently, communicating honestly, and delivering value with integrity, mission-based businesses can transform transactional relationships into enduring communities.

Authenticity, at its core, is a return to the human. It reminds us that behind every brand is a set of choices, behind every customer is a set of values, and between them lies a profound opportunity—not just to sell, but to serve. In a world where cynicism is easy and sincerity is rare, those who dare to be real will stand out—not because they're louder, but because they're trusted. And in the long game of business, trust is the only loyalty that money can't buy but mission can build.

The Pricing Paradox: How Undercharging Kills Impact

Among purpose-driven entrepreneurs, there exists a persistent and damaging myth: that to remain ethical, accessible, or mission-aligned, one must keep prices low. This belief is often rooted in noble intent—a desire to serve marginalised communities, avoid elitism, and reject the hyper-commercialism of conventional business. Yet in practice, chronically underpricing not only undermines financial sustainability but constrains impact, weakens trust, and perpetuates the very inequities many entrepreneurs set out to challenge. The paradox is clear: undercharging in the name of service often results in less service, lower quality, and faster burnout.

This mindset, while emotionally intuitive, is intellectually flawed and economically counterproductive. It conflates affordability with accessibility and assumes that price alone is the most ethical lever a founder can pull. In truth, sustainable pricing is not about extracting the maximum from every customer—it is about ensuring the business can deliver consistent value, reinvest in quality, and scale its mission without compromising the wellbeing of the entrepreneur or the integrity of the offering.

To understand how this paradox plays out, consider the case of purpose-led consultants, coaches, or creators who routinely discount their work, fearing that charging what it's worth will alienate those they seek to help. Initially, this may seem generous or humble. But over time, it leads to chronic overwork, inconsistent service, and financial instability. It becomes impossible to invest in support, infrastructure, or marketing—all of which are necessary to grow and serve more people. What began as a self-sacrificial stance becomes an unsustainable model that restricts reach and undermines the very impact the entrepreneur aspired to deliver.

The psychological drivers behind underpricing are complex. Many founders—especially women, creatives, and those from historically excluded groups—struggle with internalised beliefs around self-worth, money, and service. They fear being seen as greedy or fear criticism from their community. They equate pricing with identity, rather than positioning, and overlook the fact that price communicates more than affordability—it communicates value, quality, and commitment.

Behavioural economics supports this. Numerous studies have shown that consumers associate price with perceived value. When something is priced too low, particularly in service-based or bespoke industries, it signals lower quality—even if the product or service is objectively excellent. This creates a dangerous double bind: the business earns less while also being taken less seriously. Ironically, in trying to remain accessible, the entrepreneur creates a psychological barrier to trust and buy-in.

The issue becomes even more pronounced when viewed through the lens of impact. Every enterprise, no matter how mission-oriented, requires financial oxygen. Underpricing suffocates growth. It prevents investment in technology, talent, and innovation. It limits the ability to offer scholarships, subsidised tiers, or community programmes—tools that could *genuinely* increase accessibility. Sustainable pricing, by contrast, generates surplus that can be reinvested strategically to serve those who cannot pay without penalising those who can.

An instructive example is the business model of One Girl, an Australian non-profit that supports girls' education in Sierra Leone and Uganda. Co-founders Chantelle Baxter and Dave Dixon initially resisted applying business thinking to their organisation. But over time, they realised that relying solely on donations was precarious. They began incorporating paid speaking engagements and merchandise sales as revenue streams—not to commercialise their mission, but to sustain it. This pricing shift allowed them to grow their team, reach more girls, and build lasting partnerships. By charging where appropriate, they funded where needed.

This balance—charging in some areas to subsidise others—is central to ethical pricing. Tiered models, sliding scales, and cross-subsidisation are not new ideas, but they are underutilised in mission-driven ventures. When designed thoughtfully, these models allow for financial inclusivity without devaluing the work. They signal respect for those who pay and care for those who cannot, without compromising the business's stability. Crucially, they rely on the principle that sustainability is ethical—not selfish.

Another powerful case is that of Arlan Hamilton, founder of Backstage Capital, a venture fund dedicated to investing in underrepresented founders. Hamilton's early funding model was unconventional, relying on speaking gigs and book sales to bootstrap her firm. She charged significant fees not to enrich herself, but to fund a mission that traditional investors overlooked. Her pricing was unapologetic because it was mission-aligned. By owning the value of her work and refusing to discount it, she demonstrated that pricing can be both principled and powerful.

For entrepreneurs seeking to recalibrate their pricing without betraying their values, the first step is mindset. Pricing is not a moral judgement—it is a business strategy. Your price does not reflect your goodness, but your business model. To price ethically is not to keep prices low; it is to ensure your work is delivered at its highest quality, with sustainability, integrity, and reach. That requires factoring in your costs—not just the tangible ones like software or staff, but also your time, your expertise, and your energy. It also means understanding your market positioning and the real-world value your clients derive.

Next comes transparency. One of the most effective tools in ethical pricing is openness. Share how your pricing supports your mission. Explain what goes into delivering your service or product. When customers understand the rationale behind pricing—especially if it includes subsidising impact—they are more likely to support it. Transparency turns pricing from a barrier into a trust-building exercise. Brands like Everlane and Public Goods have built entire customer bases on this model, showing that honesty is not only ethical—it's a market differentiator.

It's also important to consider the long-term cost of underpricing—not just for the business, but for the founder. Emotional burnout, decision fatigue, and financial instability are all consequences of chronically undervaluing one's work. Over time, this depletes not only energy but creativity, leading to lower innovation and eventually to exit or failure. The impact that might have flourished under a well-capitalised, well-structured model dies quietly from overwork and under-earning.

The antidote is courageous recalibration. Entrepreneurs must be willing to raise prices when value increases, to let go of clients who do not respect the model, and to reorient their messaging around results rather than affordability. This is not arrogance—it is leadership. And in today's trust economy, leadership rooted in conviction and clarity is what builds communities, not just customers.

A final insight worth emphasising is this: pricing is not a standalone decision. It is a reflection of your business architecture, your customer strategy, and your vision for growth. When aligned with purpose and communicated with clarity, it becomes a powerful force for good—not despite its financial impact, but because of it. Sustainable pricing funds bold missions. It creates freedom. It attracts serious clients. It empowers teams. And it signals, unequivocally, that you take your work—and your impact—seriously.

Purpose-driven entrepreneurs must unlearn the idea that money corrupts meaning. Instead, they must embrace the truth that money, when earned and managed with integrity, is what *powers* meaning. It is what builds schools, funds campaigns, supports staff, and fuels the long arc of systemic change. Pricing is not a betrayal of mission. Done well, it is its most loyal ally.

Impact-Driven Business Models: How to Scale Without Losing Integrity

Scaling a business has long been associated with trade-offs—between efficiency and ethos, reach and roots, profitability and principle. For mission-driven entrepreneurs, this tension is especially acute. They enter the market not merely to capture value, but to create it—socially, environmentally, and ethically. Yet as their ventures grow, so too does the pressure to conform to conventional business norms that often prioritise speed, cost-cutting, and competitive dominance over mission fidelity. The central question, then, is not *can* a purpose-driven enterprise scale, but *how* can it do so without sacrificing the very values that underpin its existence?

The answer lies in designing impact-driven business models that do not treat purpose as an accessory to growth, but as its engine. These are models in which integrity is operationalised—embedded in pricing, supply chains, partnerships, hiring, and product development. They balance financial sustainability with value-based decision-making, proving that growth need not dilute meaning. When built with foresight and intention, these models demonstrate that scale and integrity are not mutually exclusive—they are mutually reinforcing.

One of the most celebrated examples of this principle in action is Ben & Jerry's. Founded in 1978 with a vision of community-focused capitalism, the company has consistently woven social impact into its operations—from sourcing Fairtrade-certified ingredients to championing racial justice and climate advocacy. When Unilever acquired the company in 2000, many feared its mission would be subsumed by corporate interests. But Ben & Jerry's negotiated an unusual agreement: while Unilever would manage the financial side, a separate board would oversee the company's social mission. This structural safeguard allowed Ben & Jerry's to scale globally while deepening its advocacy work. The brand's integrity not only remained intact—it became a unique value proposition that enhanced customer loyalty and attracted top-tier talent.

The lesson here is not simply to fight for a social mission clause in an acquisition deal. It is to understand that mission can and should be safeguarded through governance, legal structures, and intentional design. One increasingly popular framework for this is the benefit corporation—or B Corp—model. Certified B Corporations commit to meeting rigorous standards of social and environmental performance, accountability, and transparency. They embed impact into their legal DNA, protecting the mission even as the business attracts investment or changes leadership.

Take the example of Allbirds, the sustainable footwear company known for its use of natural materials and carbon-neutral practices. From its inception, Allbirds positioned environmental responsibility not as a marketing strategy but as a non-negotiable foundation. As the company scaled, it invested in proprietary innovations like SweetFoam—a sugarcane-based alternative to petroleum-based EVA—rather than outsourcing production to reduce costs. It also publicly disclosed its carbon footprint and invited competitors to adopt its technologies. This open-source ethos, far from diminishing its competitiveness, strengthened Allbirds' reputation and helped it expand into international markets while staying true to its core mission.

The success of such models challenges the traditional growth playbook, which assumes that scaling requires compromising on margins, diluting brand values, or adopting aggressive cost-cutting strategies. Instead, impact-driven businesses thrive by deepening alignment between values and operations. They see transparency not as a liability but as a differentiator. They view stakeholder accountability not as bureaucratic burden but as a driver of innovation and resilience.

Warby Parker offers another instructive example. The eyewear company entered a market dominated by high mark-ups and opaque pricing. Its founders chose to disrupt the industry not only through direct-to-consumer distribution but also through a "Buy a

Pair, Give a Pair" model that donates glasses to people in need. As it scaled, Warby Parker maintained a strong internal culture focused on access, equity, and design integrity. The company's social impact was not a campaign—it was built into the business model. This integration allowed it to grow rapidly while retaining public trust and employee engagement, ultimately culminating in a successful IPO without losing sight of its founding principles.

What these businesses share is not just a commitment to values, but a strategic approach to embedding those values into the mechanisms of scale. This involves more than brand storytelling—it requires structural innovation. For some, this might mean employee ownership models that redistribute wealth and decision-making. For others, it could involve supply chain localisation, regenerative practices, or customer ownership through cooperatives or community shares. The key is not the tactic itself, but the intentionality behind it: a deliberate choice to grow *with* values rather than around them.

Of course, scaling with integrity is not without its tensions. As customer bases diversify, so too do expectations. As teams grow, culture can fray. As external capital enters, the pressure to hit aggressive KPIs may clash with long-term mission goals. This is why impact-driven entrepreneurs must build robust feedback mechanisms—systems that allow them to listen, adapt, and remain accountable to the communities they serve.

One powerful tool in this regard is stakeholder mapping. Traditional businesses focus almost exclusively on shareholders; impact-led ventures take a broader view, mapping out how their decisions affect employees, customers, suppliers, communities, and the environment. This lens enables more holistic decision-making, ensuring that growth does not come at the expense of mission. It also creates a feedback loop that sharpens strategy and builds trust—an invaluable asset in a transparency-driven economy.

Consider the model employed by Tony's Chocolonely, a Dutch confectionery company on a mission to make chocolate 100% slave-free. The company has grown rapidly while maintaining a deep commitment to ethical sourcing and labour practices. Rather than simply sourcing Fairtrade cocoa, Tony's created a traceable supply chain and actively campaigns for reform in the chocolate industry. It publishes annual impact reports with detailed data and challenges competitors to follow suit. By making its entire value chain visible and accountable, Tony's has managed to scale with integrity and inspire systemic change.

There is also a cultural dimension to scaling impact. Founders must articulate not just what the business does, but what it stands for—clearly, repeatedly, and internally as much as externally. Culture is not defined by perks or slogans; it is reinforced through decisions, behaviours, and incentives. As teams grow, preserving this culture requires conscious onboarding, values-based hiring, and leadership development that emphasises emotional intelligence and systems thinking.

Ultimately, the question of how to scale without losing integrity is a question of leadership. It asks founders to resist the seduction of short-term optimisation in favour of long-term coherence. It demands a willingness to challenge industry norms, invest in mission-aligned innovation, and set a higher standard for what business can be. It invites a redefinition of success—not as revenue maximisation, but as value creation across multiple dimensions.

Impact-driven business models are not just ethically compelling—they are economically viable. They generate loyal customers, engaged employees, and resilient organisations. They foster ecosystems of trust in an era of scepticism. And they chart a path for a new kind of entrepreneurship—one that scales not by abandoning its soul, but by anchoring to it more deeply.

To scale without losing integrity is not to escape complexity. It is to embrace it. To hold tension, balance priorities, and design with discipline. It is to prove, through practice, that business can be both expansive and principled. And in doing so, it sets a precedent for the next generation of enterprises—enterprises that do not simply aim to grow, but to grow *well.*

Case Study: How a Nonprofit Founder Built a $10M Brand While Staying True to Her Mission

When most people think of nonprofits, they imagine tight budgets, grant dependency, and a constant hustle for donations—noble in intention, but rarely scalable. Yet a growing class of entrepreneurial changemakers is challenging this paradigm, demonstrating that impact-driven ventures can scale to millions in revenue *without* compromising their founding mission. Among the most compelling of these examples is the story of Leila Janah, the visionary behind Samasource, who turned a small social enterprise into a multimillion-dollar brand that transformed the tech sector—and thousands of lives—by proving that mission and market can thrive together.

Founded in 2008, Samasource began with an ambitious yet deceptively simple idea: connect people living in poverty to digital work. At a time when tech companies were outsourcing to low-cost markets with little concern for ethics or equity, Janah envisioned a model where technology could become a force for inclusion rather than exploitation. Her mission was to provide dignified, computer-based employment to those living below the poverty line—particularly women and youth in marginalised regions such as Kenya, Uganda, and India.

But unlike most traditional nonprofits, Janah refused to rely solely on donations or philanthropy. She recognised early on that for Samasource to be sustainable and credible in the competitive world of technology services, it needed to operate with the rigour and responsiveness of a for-profit enterprise. Her solution was to build a hybrid model that combined the social mission of a nonprofit with the operational discipline and revenue logic of a digital agency.

From the outset, Janah set Samasource apart by selling data annotation and content moderation services to some of the world's largest tech firms—including Google, Microsoft, and eBay. These companies had vast needs for clean, labelled data to power their artificial intelligence systems, and Samasource delivered that work with quality and reliability. The differentiator? All of it was done by people who had previously been excluded from the formal economy. Samasource trained workers from low-income communities and paid them living wages, offering not just employment but upward mobility.

This dual commitment to commercial excellence and social impact proved revolutionary. By 2019, Samasource had grown into a $10 million enterprise, employing more than 2,900 workers globally and impacting over 50,000 individuals when accounting for household benefits. What makes this trajectory extraordinary is not just the revenue figures, but how meticulously the organisation stayed anchored to its mission—even as it scaled into a player in the highly competitive tech services landscape.

One of Janah's key insights was that *mission can be a competitive advantage* if integrated authentically. Rather than soft-pedalling the company's social model, Samasource leaned into it. Clients were not merely buying a service—they were participating in a movement. The company's transparency around wages, impact metrics, and worker stories created a powerful emotional connection that resonated with clients and differentiated Samasource from faceless outsourcing giants. This moral clarity didn't diminish their market credibility—it enhanced it.

Samasource also benefited from Janah's refusal to compromise on quality. A common criticism of impact-driven enterprises is that they prioritise good intentions over performance. Janah disrupted that narrative. She insisted that her workers meet world-class standards, and she invested heavily in training, infrastructure, and quality assurance. This ensured that clients returned not out of charity, but because the product was outstanding. As she often remarked, "Giving work is better than giving aid—but only if the work is excellent."

The decision to evolve Samasource into a revenue-generating entity with a nonprofit structure was strategic and values-driven. As a nonprofit, the organisation could reinvest earnings into training programmes and worker development without pressure from shareholders. Yet it operated with the discipline of a tech start-up—measuring impact through data, iterating services based on client feedback, and maintaining lean operations. It was this rare fusion of idealism and execution that allowed Samasource to scale without mission drift.

Moreover, Janah was relentless in championing a new narrative around poverty and potential. Through her TED Talks, op-eds, and public speaking, she challenged the stereotype of people in poverty as passive recipients of aid. Instead, she framed them as underutilised talent—smart, capable individuals who simply lacked access to opportunity. This reframing was not just morally correct—it was brand-enhancing. It helped Samasource attract partnerships with progressive corporations, grants from impact investors, and talent who wanted to be part of something transformative.

Janah's legacy also lives on in the broader ecosystem she helped shape. Samaschool, a spinoff initiative, trained underserved populations in the United States to access gig economy jobs, adapting her model for domestic application. She later launched LXMI, a luxury skincare brand that sourced rare botanicals from women's co-operatives in Africa, again proving that commerce can be designed around equity, not just efficiency.

Her work anticipated a broader shift in how business, philanthropy, and social innovation intersect. She demonstrated that nonprofits can be entrepreneurial, that social impact can be measurable, and that growth does not require ethical compromise. Samasource became a blueprint for what many now refer to as the "mission economy"—an economic model where doing good is not a constraint on profitability, but a driver of it.

Of course, Janah's path was not without challenges. Balancing the demands of high-profile tech clients with the need to provide ongoing training and support to her workforce was resource-intensive. As with many impact-led models, managing expectations across stakeholders—from clients to donors to regulators—required constant negotiation and strategic clarity. Yet through it all, the organisation never lost sight of its founding question: how can we use the tools of capitalism to correct its inequities?

Perhaps the most enduring lesson from Samasource is that scale does not have to come at the cost of soul. When values are operationalised—when they inform not just branding, but hiring, pricing, partnerships, and performance—they become a source of resilience and differentiation. Samasource didn't scale by softening its mission. It scaled by hardening its systems around that mission.

Today, as more entrepreneurs seek to build ventures that are both impactful and financially viable, Janah's story serves as both inspiration and roadmap. It shows that there is a path beyond the false binary of doing good versus doing well. It reveals that nonprofit status is not a barrier to scale, and that ethics can live not just in mission statements but in balance sheets. It reminds us that with creativity, courage, and commitment, it is possible to build a $10 million brand—and a far greater legacy—without ever losing sight of why it began.

Chapter 4
The Burnout Barometer

In the purpose-first economy—where passion is prized and impact lionised—burnout has quietly crept in, unannounced but deeply entrenched. It rarely bursts onto the scene with drama. Instead, it wears the mask of dedication: *I love this work. It matters. I'm not in it for the money.* The slogans sound noble—until your chest tightens, your mornings start with dread, and the mission that once set you ablaze begins to feel oddly hollow. For founders whose businesses are built on meaning, this erosion is more than fatigue; it's a kind of existential betrayal. The very fuel becomes the fire that scorches.

This chapter opens with a challenge to the unspoken dogma of relentless grind that pervades the social impact world. Hustle, in these circles, isn't just a means—it's often mistaken for virtue. But burnout, as we'll see, isn't simply the result of working long hours. It grows from deeper soil: the emotional labour of bearing responsibility not only for a business, but for the change it promises to deliver. For many mission-led entrepreneurs, this burden is acute. They don't just want their venture to thrive—they believe it *must*, because someone's future is tethered to it. And that belief, while powerful, is what renders them so vulnerable to overreach, perfectionism, and the creeping inability to step away.

There's a seductive lie at the heart of all this: that doing what you love somehow shields you from collapse. If anything, it makes you more susceptible. A study by the Yale Center for Emotional Intelligence and the Faas Foundation highlighted that people in mission-focused roles often report both high engagement and elevated stress. Passion, it turns out, is a double-edged sword. It pushes you to deliver, to persevere—but also conceals the early signals of depletion. The descent is gradual: what once excited you starts to drain you; the people you serve begin to irritate; inspiration dries up and your work becomes procedural. You're showing up—but on autopilot.

This phenomenon—the Silent Cost of Purpose-Driven Hustle—rarely makes it into the metrics. It doesn't show up in profit-and-loss statements, nor does it break through in curated social media narratives. It accumulates quietly, insidiously. In skipped lunches. Cancelled breaks. The laptop that opens again at midnight. And it's not just physical; it's moral. When burnout is entangled with identity and purpose, healing isn't as simple as taking a weekend off. It demands a deeper reckoning—an acknowledgment of the chasm between your human limits and your boundless longing to matter.

To address this, leaders need more than wellness slogans or the occasional mindfulness app. One pragmatic tool explored in this chapter is the Energy Audit. Think of it as a diagnostic—not to count tasks completed, but to trace where your energy flows and where it leaks. How many hours actually restore you? How many obligations feel performative? This isn't about doing less; it's about realignment. The Energy Audit offers a structured way to assess whether your calendar reflects your values—or just your guilt. Where hustle turns into martyrdom, the audit shines a light.

From there, we move to a more provocative concept: Sustainable Hustle. Yes, intensity has its place. But what if we redefined high performance to include recovery? Sustainability, in this context, doesn't mean coasting or slacking off. It means creating rhythms that allow you to keep going without burning out. It means resisting the belief that exhaustion is the price of success. Drawing from research in organisational behaviour and performance science, we explore practical ways founders can hardwire rest into their workflow, delegate without shame, and—perhaps most radically—design companies that don't rely on their own superhuman effort to function.

At the heart of this reframing is a confrontation with our obsession with growth. Bigger is not always better. The chapter introduces what we call the 'Enough' Mindset—a quietly revolutionary lens that challenges the dogma of scale. Many entrepreneurs chase more—more users, more revenue, more reach—without pausing to ask: for whom? And at what cost? Growth can be good, but only when tethered to purpose. Left unchecked, it becomes a treadmill that saps meaning and breeds dysfunction. Here, we offer tools for defining what "enough" means—for your income, your team, your impact. Not as a retreat from ambition, but as a safeguard for integrity.

To anchor these reflections in action, we introduce the Burnout Barometer—an interactive self-assessment designed to reveal how aligned (or misaligned) your internal state is with your external output. It spans emotional resilience, energy allocation, time ownership, and the firmness of your boundaries. Not just a red-flag detector, the barometer is a roadmap. It offers tangible adjustments—small, implementable shifts—that recalibrate your business and restore your centre of gravity.

But let's not pretend this is just a tactical intervention. There's something quietly political about reclaiming your well-being in a world that venerates exhaustion. To rest is to dissent. To set boundaries is to lead. To say "no" is to affirm the legitimacy of your own needs—and your vision's right to longevity. Resilience, in this light, isn't about stoicism or pushing through. It's the capacity to pause, to reassess, and to return with intention.

And no, this isn't about bubble baths and journaling (though if that works for you, no judgement). It's about stewardship. You, as the founder, are not separate from your venture's mission. You *are* the conduit. If you collapse, so does the current. So protecting your energy isn't indulgence—it's infrastructure.

Throughout this chapter, we'll hear from leaders who got ahead of the collapse. Who recognised burnout before it broke them. Who retooled their work lives not just to survive, but to thrive again—with more clarity, more conviction, and fewer 2 a.m. spirals. Their stories remind us: there is no badge for self-erasure. But there *is* lasting impact to be made when sustainability is treated as strategic necessity—not after the crisis, but before it begins.

Burnout, in mission-driven ventures, is not a character flaw. It is a structural hazard, seeded by systems that privilege output over process, sacrifice over sense. This chapter is not a call to shrink your ambition, but to temper it with discernment. It's a case for working not just harder, but wiser—more attuned to your limits, and more respectful of your own humanity.

Because while purpose is meant to ignite, it should not incinerate. The flame must be managed—fed, shielded, kept steady. The Burnout Barometer is an invitation: to build not just with fervour, but with foresight. Not just to go far, but to go well.

The Silent Cost of Purpose-Driven Hustle

There is a certain reverence with which society views purpose-driven work. Those who commit their lives to solving social problems, uplifting communities, or championing causes are often seen as moral beacons—individuals fuelled by conviction rather than compensation, grit rather than gain. Yet beneath this admiration lies a dangerous assumption: that purpose is protection. That because mission-driven individuals care deeply about their work, they are somehow more resilient, more immune to exhaustion, more capable of pushing through. This belief, while seductive, is catastrophically false. In fact, research and lived experience consistently reveal that purpose-driven individuals are *more* vulnerable to burnout, not less.

The paradox of purpose is that it energises and erodes in equal measure. On one hand, it offers meaning, direction, and identity. On the other, it creates an emotional entanglement with work that makes rest feel like abandonment, delegation feel like dilution, and slowing down feel like failure. Unlike conventional burnout—often caused by toxic workplaces, meaningless tasks, or misaligned roles—purpose-driven burnout is more insidious. It is the slow erosion of vitality under the weight of one's own ideals.

What makes this phenomenon particularly complex is that it often masquerades as engagement. The person experiencing it may appear passionate, prolific, and committed on the outside, while internally they are hollowing out. The language of mission—*this work matters*, *people are counting on me*, *I can't stop now*—can obscure early warning signs, allowing burnout to incubate unnoticed. And because these individuals are often the founders, leaders, or cultural anchors of their organisations, the cost of their decline is not only personal—it reverberates across teams, stakeholders, and impact outcomes.

A study conducted by the University of California, Berkeley, found that non-profit and social enterprise workers exhibit some of the highest levels of emotional exhaustion across any professional sector. The combination of high personal investment, ambiguous success metrics, and resource constraints creates a pressure cooker environment where overwork is normalised and self-care is pathologised as selfishness. Founders, in particular, report feeling unable to step back for fear of stalling momentum or disappointing beneficiaries, funders, or communities. The result is what organisational psychologist Dr Christina Maslach terms *moral burnout*—a form of emotional depletion that occurs when the desire to help becomes a source of distress.

Consider the story of Sarah Corbett, founder of the Craftivist Collective in the UK. What began as a quiet, values-led movement to use craft as a tool for activism gained widespread attention, partnerships with global charities, and growing public expectations. Though the movement retained its integrity, Corbett found herself grappling with the relentless emotional and logistical demands of scaling a cause without losing its soul. Eventually, she publicly addressed her experience with burnout—not as a cautionary tale of failure, but as a necessary conversation about boundaries, sustainability, and the mythology of the tireless changemaker. Her story, like so many others, reveals a truth we often avoid: passion is not infinite. Without containment, it becomes combustion.

So what are the early signs that purpose-driven individuals may be on a path to depletion?

One of the first is *numbing*. Whereas burnout in traditional settings often manifests as overt irritability or absenteeism, mission-driven burnout can begin with subtle emotional blunting. Tasks that once inspired joy feel perfunctory. Compassion becomes performative. The founder who once wrote fundraising emails with heartfelt conviction now dreads every send. The coach who once found deep meaning in client transformation begins to feel indifferent.

This detachment is not laziness—it is a protective response to chronic emotional overexposure.

Another sign is *rigid overfunctioning*. Rather than stepping back when overwhelmed, the purpose-driven individual leans in harder—taking on more roles, refusing to rest, micromanaging every outcome. This behaviour is often rooted in a fear that others will not carry the mission with the same integrity or intensity. Ironically, this hyper-control often erodes the collaborative culture necessary for true impact. Teams become disempowered, succession planning is neglected, and the founder becomes the single point of failure in a system that cannot sustain itself.

Sleep disturbances, anxiety spikes, and somatic symptoms such as headaches, digestive issues, or chronic fatigue are also common. These physiological cues often precede conscious awareness. Because purpose-driven individuals are so attuned to their mission, they may ignore what their bodies are trying to communicate. They'll rationalise it—*I'm just tired*, *this is a big launch*, *next quarter will be better*—until the symptoms become impossible to ignore.

The most dangerous sign, however, is the erosion of *joy*. When purpose becomes pressure, when mission becomes a mandate rather than a choice, even the most values-aligned work loses its aliveness. The individual no longer connects to the *why* that once fuelled them. Instead, they feel trapped by it. This emotional dislocation is particularly distressing because it strikes at the heart of identity. If the thing that once gave your life meaning now feels burdensome, who are you without it?

What can be done to intervene before burnout metastasises?

The first step is recognition. This may sound obvious, but it is perhaps the hardest task for the mission-led individual who sees discomfort as part of the deal. Normalising conversations around burnout—not as failure but as feedback—creates psychological safety. Leaders must model vulnerability and invite it in others. Boards must ask not just about impact metrics, but about founder well-being. Donors must respect boundaries, not reward burnout.

The second is recalibration. Burnout is rarely solved by a weekend off or a yoga retreat. It requires systemic shifts in how time, energy, and expectations are managed. This might include restructuring roles to align with actual capacity, building in recovery cycles after major launches, or implementing "mission audits" to ensure that the work being done still aligns with the values it purports to serve. In some cases, it may require stepping away entirely—at least temporarily—to rediscover clarity, capacity, and perspective.

The third is redefining success. Too often, purpose-led ventures borrow growth metrics from traditional business models without questioning whether those metrics align with sustainability or integrity. Founders chase scale, media attention, or revenue targets that were never part of the original mission. Reclaiming agency over what *enough* looks like is one of the most subversive acts a mission-led entrepreneur can undertake. It restores autonomy, honours the finite nature of human energy, and preserves the quality of impact over its quantity.

Finally, it is vital to build support structures that are not conditional on performance. Many purpose-driven individuals receive validation only when they are "doing good" or producing results. This creates a feedback loop where identity becomes tethered to output. Friends, therapists, mentors, and peers who can hold space for the *person*, not just the mission, are essential. No one should have to earn rest. No one should have to justify their limits.

The silent cost of purpose-driven hustle is not just burnout—it is the loss of leaders who once saw clearly and loved deeply. It is the dilution of missions that become mechanised. It is the erosion of trust in movements that cannot sustain themselves. But it is also avoidable. By bringing awareness, systems, and compassion to the way we build and lead, we can create a new paradigm—one where sustainability is not an afterthought, but a foundation.

Because purpose should be a source of power, not depletion. And to honour it fully, we must protect the people who carry it. Not by asking them to do more with less, but by giving them the space to breathe, the permission to rest, and the support to thrive—long after the initial fire of passion has settled into something quieter, but infinitely more enduring.

The Energy Audit: Tracking Your Passion vs. Exhaustion Ratio

For purpose-driven entrepreneurs, the metric of progress has traditionally been external: number of clients served, funds raised, impact reports compiled, social media traction, revenue milestones. These are important indicators of influence and reach, but they often fail to capture what is quietly happening inside the person at the centre of it all. While the world sees outputs, the entrepreneur experiences inputs—an ongoing exchange of time, emotion, and cognitive labour that determines not just productivity but sustainability. It is within this exchange that the *Energy Audit* becomes essential: a structured, introspective tool to track how your work affects you on an emotional and psychological level, and to illuminate the ratio between passion and exhaustion before depletion becomes dysfunction.

At its essence, the Energy Audit is a diagnostic process—part reflective practice, part behavioural inventory—that invites founders and leaders to assess their daily activities not by financial yield or perceived importance, but by their energetic return. It asks a simple yet profound question: does this work give me energy, or take it away?

This is not about hedonism or ease. Not all energising tasks are comfortable, and not all draining ones are unworthy. But over time, a consistent tilt towards depletion, without counterbalancing renewal, leads to burnout—not only of the body, but of motivation, clarity, and mission. The Energy Audit is a tool to surface the hidden economics of your energy expenditure, to spot patterns that undermine your wellbeing, and to design your workload in a way that honours both your mission and your limits.

The need for such a tool arises from the unique way purpose-driven people engage with their work. When your work is closely tied to your values, your identity, and your personal narrative, every win feels deeply affirming—but every obstacle cuts deeper too.

Unlike purely commercial entrepreneurs who may pursue exit strategies or delegate for efficiency, mission-led founders often wear every operational inefficiency, client disappointment, or policy hurdle as a personal failure. Their to-do lists are not just tasks; they are threads connected to lives, systems, and legacies. In this context, traditional productivity tools that prioritise output optimisation are not enough. What's needed is a way to measure the *emotional ROI* of the work.

A growing body of research supports the relevance of energy over time as a performance metric. Psychologist Jim Loehr and performance expert Tony Schwartz, in their work with elite athletes and executives, found that high achievement was less about the number of hours worked and more about the management of energy across four domains: physical, emotional, mental, and spiritual. Their framework suggests that burnout occurs not from stress itself, but from the absence of adequate recovery. The Energy Audit translates this insight into practical application for mission-led professionals, providing a mechanism to track energy outputs and design workflows that sustain rather than drain.

To begin the process, one must first develop the habit of observation. This involves tracking your day in blocks and noting how each activity makes you feel—not just whether you completed it, but how you felt before, during, and after. Was it mentally taxing? Did it provoke anxiety or enthusiasm? Did you feel creatively stimulated or emotionally depleted? These reflections need not be lengthy, but they must be honest. Over time, patterns emerge. Perhaps client calls, though time-consuming, leave you feeling connected and fulfilled. Perhaps email triage, while easy, creates a slow-drip dread. Perhaps public speaking energises you more than you expected, while strategic planning—previously thought of as essential CEO work—consistently drains your clarity.

This exercise forces a reconceptualisation of time. It shifts the focus from how long something takes to how deeply it affects you. Time, after all, is a fixed resource; energy is renewable but finite. A task that consumes an hour and energises you is very different from one that takes 30 minutes but leaves you depleted for the rest of the day. When decision-making is guided by energy data, not just time efficiency, leaders make more sustainable choices. They begin to protect their most generative hours and design workflows that match their natural rhythms, rather than contorting themselves into the mould of what productivity is "supposed" to look like.

The Energy Audit also provides a corrective to the myth of equal weighting. Many entrepreneurs treat all tasks as equally important—especially in early-stage ventures where bootstrapping means doing everything. But not all tasks are equal in their energetic cost. Answering a tense investor email may seem small in the scheme of things, but if it creates three hours of rumination and self-doubt, its true cost is invisible but immense. Likewise, facilitating a creative team session may take half a day, but if it re-anchors you in purpose and vision, it may offset multiple draining tasks. The goal is not to avoid hard work, but to ensure that the energy investments yield returns—emotionally, intellectually, or relationally.

Consider the example of Whitney Bauck, a journalist and climate advocate who consciously tracks her energy fluctuations across work assignments. She discovered that investigative reporting, while highly meaningful, required more emotional recovery time than opinion writing, and that fieldwork invigorated her far more than virtual panels. By identifying these trends, she was able to design her schedule to alternate heavy and light tasks, reduce emotional whiplash, and build in micro-recoveries between intensive work periods. The result was not less productivity, but more sustainable output, less emotional volatility, and a deepened connection to her mission.

Similarly, in the start-up world, Tristan Walker—founder of Walker & Company Brands—famously restructured his day around high-energy periods, preserving mornings for creative and strategic tasks and avoiding emotionally charged meetings in the afternoon. For Walker, protecting his energy was not a luxury; it was a leadership imperative. His clarity, patience, and vision were directly tied to how well he managed his inputs, not just his calendar.

For the Energy Audit to be useful, it must also inform real behavioural shifts. Awareness is only the first step. The next is rebalancing: increasing the ratio of energising activities relative to draining ones, and inserting intentional recovery into high-output phases. This might involve outsourcing a task that, while simple, creates a disproportionate drag. It could mean rearranging meetings so that energising collaborations offset difficult negotiations. It could mean giving yourself permission to say no to opportunities that look good on paper but cost more than they return.

This is not an exercise in fragility. On the contrary, it is a practice of resilience. Leaders who regularly conduct energy audits tend to notice burnout earlier, recover faster, and make more courageous strategic decisions. They are better able to differentiate between stress that signals growth and stress that signals harm. They are less reactive, more reflective, and more attuned to the subtle signals of misalignment that precede bigger ruptures.

The Energy Audit also intersects with the growing movement toward trauma-informed entrepreneurship—a recognition that many founders carry psychological wounds from systemic marginalisation, family history, or previous burnout. These individuals are often hyper-capable, but operate with a constant low-grade anxiety that skews their perception of capacity. For them, the audit can be a revelation: an evidence-based way to challenge internalised narratives of not doing enough, and to design from wholeness rather than fear.

Over time, the audit becomes less a worksheet and more a mindset—a way of approaching work with curiosity and compassion. It fosters a new form of literacy: energetic literacy. Leaders begin to sense when their enthusiasm is no longer authentic, when tension in the body precedes a decision misaligned with values, or when their best contributions are being undermined by cumulative fatigue. This literacy does not replace strategy—it sharpens it. It ensures that the person at the helm remains connected, conscious, and capable of sustaining the impact they've set out to create.

To measure your life's work only by the metrics visible to others is to risk eroding the invisible structures that make it possible: clarity, vitality, discernment, joy. The Energy Audit returns agency to the individual—not to escape responsibility, but to deepen it. Because the most sustainable impact is not created by those who push endlessly forward, but by those who know when to pause, assess, and protect the source of their own fire.

When founders learn to track their energy with the same fidelity they track their revenue, they build companies that last—not because they avoided exhaustion, but because they chose awareness. Not because they were unbreakable, but because they were wise enough to stop before they shattered. The Energy Audit is not merely a productivity tool—it is a compass for integrity, wholeness, and longevity in the work that matters most.

Sustainable Hustle: The Art of Hard Work Without Self-Destruction

The word "hustle" has undergone a curious evolution. Once associated with energetic effort and scrappy ambition, it is now canonised in entrepreneurial circles as a badge of honour—evidence of devotion, productivity, and the willingness to do whatever it takes. But beneath the sheen of motivational slogans and late-night emails lies a shadow few are willing to confront: when hustle becomes habitual, unexamined, and unrelenting, it morphs from virtue into vice. Particularly for mission-driven individuals, whose work is rooted not just in goals but in values, the cost of unsustainable hustle is not simply personal. It is strategic, cultural, and systemic.

This chapter explores the concept of *sustainable hustle*—the disciplined practice of working hard without eroding the very foundations of your long-term impact. It challenges the binary between drive and balance and reframes work-life sustainability as an act of leadership, not luxury. At its heart, sustainable hustle is about *how* we work: with rhythm, awareness, and integrity, rather than adrenaline, guilt, or self-neglect.

The psychological pull of hustle is deeply ingrained, especially in mission-driven sectors. There is an implicit moral pressure that accompanies purposeful work—the sense that because the cause matters, we must always be available, always pushing, always sacrificing. This creates a unique form of overidentification between self-worth and productivity. The mission isn't a job—it's a reflection of who you are. This makes boundaries porous and rest feel indulgent.

Yet the very logic of hustle is flawed. A growing body of evidence in organisational psychology and neuroscience confirms what lived experience already knows: prolonged overwork leads to cognitive depletion, decision fatigue, diminished creativity, and emotional burnout. The brain, much like the body, thrives on cycles of effort and recovery. Without intentional recovery, even the most resilient individuals become reactive, rigid, and prone to tunnel vision. For entrepreneurs whose ventures depend on clarity of purpose, strategic thinking, and emotional resonance, these are not minor setbacks. They are existential risks.

In contrast, sustainable hustle draws from a different operational philosophy—one that integrates intensity with intentionality. It allows for high engagement without chronic depletion. It acknowledges the necessity of effort but situates it within a structure that honours capacity, context, and seasonality.

This model is not theoretical. Consider the example of Jacinda Ardern, the former Prime Minister of New Zealand, who became internationally admired not only for her leadership during crises but for her open acknowledgment of exhaustion and her eventual resignation. Ardern did not collapse in scandal or incompetence—she stepped back at the height of her career, stating she "no longer felt she could do the job justice." Her departure was not a failure but a recalibration, a conscious act of sustainability that sparked global conversations about what responsible leadership can look like. Her decision underscored a profound truth: effectiveness is not the same as endurance.

Sustainable hustle requires a shift from linear productivity to cyclical productivity. Just as athletes periodise their training to alternate between load and recovery, so too must mission-driven professionals structure their work to account for rhythms—of the body, the team, the market, and the mission itself. This involves designing workflows that build in breathing space, intentionally punctuating high-stakes periods with active restoration. It's not just about working *less*, but about working *differently*—with strategic sprints, deliberate pauses, and a clear sense of priorities.

One practical application of this approach comes from the design firm IDEO, known for embedding "project sabbaticals" into long-term workflows. After intense innovation cycles, team members are encouraged to step back, explore creative pursuits, or shift roles. This not only prevents burnout but fuels fresh thinking and deeper cross-pollination. Their approach reflects a key insight: recovery is not a break from impact—it is a precondition for it.

On an individual level, sustainable hustle requires internal clarity around what fuels you versus what drains you. As explored in the previous subchapter on the Energy Audit, different tasks have different energetic signatures. Effective leaders curate their calendars not just for efficiency but for resonance—placing their most meaningful, generative work at the centre, and designing around it with deliberate constraints. They develop systems that protect their focus, such as time-blocking, digital boundaries, or delegation frameworks—not to avoid responsibility, but to honour their highest leverage zones.

Perhaps most importantly, sustainable hustle rests on a redefinition of success. The dominant entrepreneurial culture still privileges scale, speed, and visibility. But mission-led entrepreneurs are increasingly rewriting these metrics to include wellbeing, relational health, and mission coherence. This recalibration is evident in the rise of "slow business" movements, where companies explicitly choose measured growth, stakeholder balance, and deep community integration over hyper-scaling.

A compelling example is the social enterprise *Thankyou* in Australia, co-founded by Daniel Flynn. Initially pursuing rapid expansion through supermarkets and global licensing, the brand made a radical pivot: pulling its bestselling product line off the shelves to regain strategic control and re-align with its purpose. The decision appeared commercially risky, but it allowed the organisation to rebuild infrastructure, deepen partnerships, and re-enter the market on more sustainable terms. Flynn later described this not as stepping back, but as stepping *into* integrity. It was sustainable hustle in action—courageous, measured, and mission-first.

Sustainable hustle also invites a cultural shift within organisations. When leaders model recovery, set humane expectations, and reward consistency over heroic effort, they create environments where teams thrive over the long haul. In cultures that glorify sacrifice, burnout becomes a status symbol. In cultures that centre sustainability, wellbeing becomes a strategic asset. Psychological safety increases. Retention improves. Creativity flourishes.

This is especially critical in purpose-led ventures, where emotional labour is often high and the line between personal and professional is blurry. Teams need more than wellness webinars and HR handbooks—they need leaders who walk the talk. Who take leave, say no, and create space for others to do the same without fear of being seen as less committed. As researcher and author Brené Brown puts it, "You can't take people further than you're willing to go yourself." Sustainability, in this sense, is not just a policy—it's a praxis.

Still, implementing sustainable hustle requires confronting some uncomfortable myths. That we are indispensable. That if we pause, the work will suffer. That burnout is a rite of passage. These beliefs are not only inaccurate—they are harmful. They keep leaders trapped in cycles of depletion and prevent teams from maturing into adaptive, resilient organisms. The antidote is not withdrawal, but wisdom. A willingness to re-pattern our assumptions about time, energy, and value.

Ultimately, sustainable hustle is a strategic commitment to longevity. It is about building companies and careers that can withstand volatility, weather complexity, and grow roots rather than just branches. It's the art of showing up fully, repeatedly, and meaningfully—not in sprints that flame out, but in seasons that evolve. It recognises that the real test of leadership is not how much you can do, but how well you can sustain your impact without losing yourself in the process.

Mission-led work asks for a lot. But it cannot ask for everything. The work is important. But so are you. And in a world that desperately needs durable leaders—whole, well, and awake—the most radical act may be to hustle with heart *and* with balance. Not because the work is easy, but because it matters too much to burn out before it's done.

The 'Enough' Mindset: Knowing When to Scale and When to Slow Down

In a culture fixated on acceleration, bigger is often equated with better. Entrepreneurs are conditioned to chase scale—more customers, more funding, more visibility—as a proxy for success. Yet this relentless pursuit, though common, is not always strategic. For mission-driven founders especially, the assumption that growth is inherently good can quietly erode the very values their enterprises are built upon. At the intersection of purpose and profit, a different kind of discipline is required: the discernment to know not just how to grow, but *when to stop*. This is the heart of the 'Enough' mindset—a financial and strategic framework that prioritises sufficiency, sustainability, and alignment over unchecked expansion.

To embrace the 'Enough' mindset is not to reject ambition. It is to reframe it. It is a refusal to let external expectations dictate internal metrics. It is the conscious act of defining success on your own terms, in service of a life and a business that is not just scalable, but stable, values-aligned, and ultimately fulfilling. For many impact-led entrepreneurs, this shift can be both liberating and terrifying. It means measuring growth not just in terms of income or market share, but in terms of energy balance, mission fidelity, and the quality of relationships with stakeholders. It demands a deeper engagement with the question: "What are we actually building, and why?"

Financial planning within this paradigm requires clarity, nuance, and a strong sense of context. Unlike traditional growth models, which rely on aggressive projections and market dominance strategies, the 'Enough' approach is guided by intentionality. It begins with understanding your *real* needs—personally, organisationally, and mission-wise. This means developing a financial plan that supports your desired lifestyle, sustains your team without overextending them, funds your impact work at a meaningful level, and allows for reinvestment and resilience. Anything beyond that is optional, not obligatory.

This recalibration of financial goals is more than philosophical. It has practical implications for pricing, staffing, investment, and pace. Take the example of Basecamp, the software company founded by Jason Fried and David Heinemeier Hansson. For years, Basecamp has resisted venture capital, scaled its team modestly, and capped the size of its client base to ensure product quality and team wellbeing. Their revenues are substantial, their brand is trusted, and their culture is famously human-centric. They've achieved what many start-ups dream of—without chasing unicorn status. Their philosophy? "We have enough. We don't need to conquer every market. We want to do good work, pay people well, and enjoy our lives."

This philosophy requires founders to challenge internalised narratives of scarcity and inadequacy. So much of modern entrepreneurship is driven by fear—fear of being left behind, of appearing small, of missing the next big opportunity. But the data shows that exponential growth often brings exponential complexity. Costs rise, culture fragments, and the margin for error shrinks. For mission-driven ventures, which often operate with leaner teams and deeper stakeholder commitments, these dynamics can dilute impact and introduce ethical compromises.

A sustainable financial plan within the 'Enough' mindset involves three core practices: defining thresholds, building buffers, and modelling different futures. Defining thresholds means identifying the minimum viable financial outcomes that support your mission and personal wellbeing. It includes drawing a clear line between wants and needs, both emotionally and economically. Founders who know what enough looks like are less susceptible to panic pivots or shiny-object distractions. They can say no with conviction. They can pace themselves strategically rather than constantly reacting.

Building buffers is the act of designing for volatility. Purpose-led businesses, especially those working in emerging or underserved markets, are subject to more fluctuations than traditional enterprises. Cash flow may be irregular, impact work may be harder to monetise, and client acquisition cycles may be longer. Buffering for these realities—through diversified income streams, cash reserves, or flexible staffing models—frees the founder from constant survival mode and opens space for reflection and strategic clarity. It allows the business to pause, regroup, and evolve without being beholden to urgent financial pressures.

Modelling different futures is an exercise in scenario planning that avoids rigidity. Rather than assuming a single path forward, mission-driven leaders are encouraged to build several models: a conservative model that ensures survival and stability; an aspirational model that explores scale with integrity; and a retreat model that outlines what pulling back would look like if necessary. These models act as guardrails, allowing for confident decision-making even in uncertainty. They also reinforce the idea that stepping back is not always regression—it can be strategic repositioning.

A striking example of this mindset at work comes from Ali Partovi, co-founder of Code.org, a non-profit that aims to make computer science education accessible to all students. While Code.org has experienced significant growth, it has repeatedly opted for measured scaling over rapid expansion. Partovi has publicly stated that the organisation turns away funding when it risks diverting them from core focus. This kind of fiscal discipline—saying no to money that doesn't serve the mission—is a rare and powerful act. It reflects a leadership culture that prioritises coherence over capital, and recognises that more funding is not always better funding.

The 'Enough' mindset also redefines the pace of progress. In a world obsessed with quarterly results and year-over-year growth, slowing down can feel counterintuitive. But many of the most enduring and impactful organisations—whether Patagonia, Mozilla, or The Centre for Humane Technology—have grown deliberately. They have taken time to build culture, iterate on product, and forge meaningful relationships with stakeholders. They have scaled not by accelerating mindlessly, but by moving with precision and purpose. Their growth curves may be less dramatic, but they are far more sustainable.

For founders, adopting this mindset requires a new kind of courage. It means stepping away from the treadmill of endless optimisation and tuning into deeper metrics: how energised you feel, how aligned your work is with your values, how much space you have to think, connect, and evolve. It means surrounding yourself with advisors who respect sustainability, not just speed. It means holding yourself accountable not only to your mission, but to the long-term health of the ecosystem you are helping to shape.

Financially, it also means becoming fluent in the language of intentional trade-offs. You may choose slower revenue growth to maintain product quality. You may hire fewer people but pay them better. You may forgo international expansion to preserve cultural intimacy. These decisions are not signs of small thinking—they are acts of mature leadership. They reflect a commitment to building something that lasts.

Ultimately, the 'Enough' mindset is an act of resistance—against extractive capitalism, against performative entrepreneurship, against the belief that you must always be chasing something just out of reach. It's also a profound act of self-trust. To know when to scale and when to slow down is to trust your instincts, your numbers, and your deeper vision. It is to believe that you are not falling behind just because you are not racing ahead.

This mindset, when embraced collectively, could change the culture of entrepreneurship. It would create companies that grow with care, leaders who sleep at night, and missions that endure not because they were hyped, but because they were held with integrity. And perhaps most importantly, it would remind all of us that enough is not a limit. It is a strategy. A choice. A declaration that we are building not for applause, but for impact—and for the kind of success that feels whole.

Interactive Exercise: Your Burnout Barometer Score

Burnout is rarely a sudden collapse. More often, it is a gradual unraveling—one that begins in the quiet erosion of enthusiasm, in the small compromises we justify in the name of progress, and in the accumulating tension that becomes the background noise of our professional lives. For mission-driven entrepreneurs, the risk is particularly acute. Their work is not merely a job; it is an expression of identity, ethics, and purpose. This entanglement makes it difficult to discern where commitment ends and overextension begins. The *Burnout Barometer Score* is designed to interrupt that ambiguity, offering a reflective tool that not only diagnoses burnout risk, but helps reframe success through the lens of sustainability.

This interactive self-assessment is not a gimmick. It draws on decades of clinical research, behavioural science, and organisational psychology. It is rooted in the understanding that burnout manifests across multiple dimensions—emotional, physical, cognitive, and existential. The aim is to move beyond binary thinking—burned out or not burned out—and instead offer a nuanced spectrum that helps you understand your specific risk profile, your stress triggers, and your recovery patterns. From there, you can design a tailored action plan that addresses not only what's happening, but *why*.

The need for such a tool has never been greater. A 2021 McKinsey report found that 49% of workers across sectors reported feeling at least somewhat burned out. Among social impact leaders, the rate was significantly higher—over 60%, according to research from the Skoll Foundation. Yet these figures only scratch the surface. Many founders and impact professionals don't identify as burned out because they are still performing. They are delivering results, meeting deadlines, showing up. But performance under duress is not resilience; it is a warning sign. The Burnout Barometer helps surface that warning before breakdown becomes inevitable.

The structure of the assessment revolves around five key domains: energy, clarity, boundaries, emotional regulation, and mission connection. Each domain contains diagnostic questions, which, when answered honestly, provide insight into where you are operating from strength and where subtle risk is accruing. For instance, the energy domain evaluates how often you feel physically and mentally replenished after a day's work. The clarity domain explores cognitive fog, decision fatigue, and strategic drift. Boundaries assesses your ability to protect time, attention, and recovery. Emotional regulation measures mood volatility, irritability, and overwhelm. Mission connection explores your current sense of meaning and whether your work still resonates.

While a formal version of this tool includes quantifiable scoring, the deeper value lies in the qualitative insights. One of the most profound benefits of self-assessment is that it slows you down. It forces you to look inward, to translate vague discomfort into actionable understanding. You begin to notice patterns. Perhaps your exhaustion isn't just about long hours, but about how little of your time is spent on energising work. Perhaps your decision fatigue stems from unclear priorities or blurred team roles. Perhaps your emotional volatility is less about workload and more about cumulative dissonance—between your values and the choices you feel forced to make.

Take the example of Erin, a social enterprise founder working in sustainable fashion. On the outside, her business was thriving: expanding product lines, securing funding, receiving media coverage. But internally, she was nearing collapse. Through the burnout barometer, she realised her exhaustion wasn't primarily physical—it was emotional. She felt disconnected from her creative roots, overwhelmed by operational demands, and guilty for resenting the very success she had fought to build. Her assessment revealed two high-risk areas: boundary erosion and loss of mission connection. With that clarity, she made a series of changes—delegating operations, re-engaging with product design, and blocking non-negotiable recovery days. Within three months, her energy returned. More importantly, so did her joy.

These insights don't just serve individuals; they are strategic assets for the business. When leaders operate at or near burnout, decision quality declines. Vision narrows. Innovation slows. Culture suffers. By contrast, when founders understand and manage their burnout risk, they make more courageous decisions, model healthier norms, and build more resilient organisations. Self-care ceases to be an isolated activity—it becomes part of enterprise risk management.

Creating a personalised action plan begins with identifying your highest-risk domain. This is the area where you score lowest or feel most friction. From there, the plan involves three types of interventions: restorative, structural, and strategic.

Restorative interventions target immediate energy recovery—sleep, hydration, movement, and downtime. They are foundational, yet often deprioritised by high-performers. Without these in place, no productivity system will be effective. Structural interventions address the design of your workload—calendar architecture, delegation systems, communication norms. These changes require intention and sometimes negotiation, but they produce outsized returns. Strategic interventions focus on alignment—revisiting your why, rearticulating your vision, and saying no to opportunities that don't serve your long game.

An instructive case is that of Bryan Stevenson, the renowned public interest lawyer and founder of the Equal Justice Initiative. Stevenson's work is emotionally taxing by any standard. He routinely confronts injustice, trauma, and systemic oppression. And yet, he has managed to sustain this work for decades without burning out. His strategy is not mystical. It is grounded in clarity, rhythm, and purpose. He maintains deep spiritual and artistic practices, builds restorative time into his schedule, and delegates operational control to trusted lieutenants. He is deeply immersed in the mission—but not consumed by it. His approach exemplifies what burnout researcher Dr. Christina Maslach calls "sustainable engagement"—a model where intensity is metabolised through rhythm and purpose.

It's also important to recognise that burnout risk fluctuates with context. Launch phases, funding cycles, public crises—all introduce new stressors. The Burnout Barometer is not a one-time tool, but a recurring check-in. Just as businesses review their financial statements quarterly, founders should review their wellbeing profile at regular intervals. Doing so destigmatises emotional tracking and reinforces the message that self-assessment is a strength, not a weakness.

Founders who consistently use this tool report increased agency, not just over their schedules, but over their narratives. They stop seeing stress as a personal failing and start viewing it as data. They develop greater compassion for themselves and deeper empathy for their teams. And they stop assuming that sustainability is something they'll address *after* they succeed, and instead integrate it into the *way* they succeed.

This is the quiet power of the Burnout Barometer: it gives you language for what you've been sensing but unable to articulate. It turns vague exhaustion into specific insight. It allows you to step back without stepping away. And in doing so, it helps you build a business that doesn't just survive adversity, but flourishes because it is rooted in wisdom.

Burnout is not a badge of honour. It is a signal—one that, if heeded early, can catalyse transformation. The Burnout Barometer is not a cure, but a compass. It points you back to the centre, back to the question that matters most: *What does it look like to do this work in a way that is sustainable, meaningful, and whole?* If you can answer that—and build from it—then you are not merely avoiding burnout. You are modelling a new paradigm of leadership. One that lasts. One that leads with care. One that can go the distance without losing its soul.

Chapter 5
The Science of Impact-Driven Decision Making

Every entrepreneurial journey, at its heart, is stitched together by decisions—some strategic, some deeply personal, others quietly philosophical. Yet for mission-driven founders, each choice carries a particular gravity. These aren't just business calls about efficiency or revenue—they're moments of alignment, where the implications ripple beyond the balance sheet and into the moral and cultural footprint a venture leaves behind. While traditional enterprises often race ahead with a singular focus on speed or scalability, impact-led businesses navigate a denser, more intricate landscape. Success here isn't measured only by numbers—but by nuance, coherence, and conscience. This chapter sets out a framework for navigating that terrain—not by simplifying it, but by engaging with its depth.

Modern decision science has drawn from a rich blend of behavioural economics, neurobiology, and organisational psychology. Yet, for all its sophistication, the mainstream advice tends to orbit quantifiables: KPIs, shareholder returns, margins. In contrast, purpose-led ventures deal in currencies less easily measured. The question isn't just "What will this decision yield?" but "What will it cost, morally, culturally, energetically?" For these leaders, the task is to weave together instinct, data, and values into a kind of internal decision architecture—sturdy enough to hold under pressure, but flexible enough to respond to uncertainty.

Enter the Values Compass—a deceptively simple tool that invites founders to draw their own line in the sand. Built on foundations from moral psychology and value-based leadership, this compass helps leaders articulate what they will not sacrifice, regardless of external pressures. Radical transparency? Worker equity? Carbon neutrality? Whatever the principles, defining them early creates a buffer against mission drift. In the fog of rapid growth or crisis, this compass offers not certainty, but clarity—a subtle but vital distinction.

It becomes indispensable during scale-ups, partnerships, or the sharp pivots crises often demand. Take, for instance, Tony's Chocolonely—a brand that scaled internationally without backing down from its no-slavery pledge in its cocoa supply chain. At every junction—be it fundraising, marketing, or sourcing—the question was not just "Is this viable?" but "Does this align?" Their refusal to compromise became their signature. Integrity, it turns out, can be a formidable asset when demonstrated consistently.

Still, principles alone don't solve the puzzle. Decisions happen in the real world—where budgets are finite, teams are stretched, and time is in short supply. That's where a shift from thinking in terms of opportunity cost to understanding true cost proves critical. Standard ROI assessments are narrow; they don't account for the less visible, but equally consequential, costs: emotional exhaustion, cultural erosion, or reputational risk. Say yes to a contract that burns out your team or bends your standards—what's the real price?

Reframing the analysis to include these intangible, long-tail consequences can change everything. What seems irrational in a spreadsheet may, in a broader view, be an act of strategic preservation. And conversely, an "efficient" choice may later reveal itself as a form of self-sabotage. It requires a broader calculus, one that invites imagination alongside logic—and a tolerance for short-term ambiguity in pursuit of long-term coherence.

To bring order to this messier kind of discernment, traditional frameworks like the Eisenhower Matrix can be repurposed. Originally designed to sort tasks into "urgent" and "important," the matrix becomes more meaningful when reinterpreted through a values lens. Urgency, in an impact context, may not be about deadlines—it might be about mission fidelity. Importance isn't just scale; it could be about narrative integrity or community trust. By shifting the axis of evaluation, founders can better distinguish not just what clamours loudest, but what matters most.

But let's be honest—there's only so much that logic will give you. Neuroscience has long confirmed that our decisions are not, and never have been, entirely rational. The emotional brain—the ventromedial prefrontal cortex, specifically—plays a key role in judgement. In other words, the infamous "gut feeling" isn't just folklore. It's biology. The trouble is, intuition can be wise—or wildly misleading. Fatigue, ego, past wounds—they all muddy the waters.

And so arises one of the hardest balancing acts for purpose-led founders: Gut vs. Data. On one hand, visionaries often sense what's coming before anyone else sees it. On the other, instinct is easily warped. Meanwhile, data—while seemingly objective—is always partial, always filtered. The real craft is in weaving the two: knowing when to lean into a hunch, when to interrogate it, and when to anchor it with hard evidence.

We saw this artful synthesis in the work of Tensie Whelan, who, while leading the Rainforest Alliance, orchestrated a controversial merger with UTZ. Critics feared the consolidation would dilute the mission. Whelan didn't ignore those concerns—she surfaced them, investigated them. Her instincts told her the merger could magnify their reach; data, drawn from performance benchmarks and partner feedback, supported her claim. In the end, the decision proved transformative, unifying two major players into a force that redefined global sustainability standards. The lesson? Trust your gut—but bring receipts.

The chapter's final section grounds these ideas in a detailed case study: a founder who walked away from a lucrative acquisition deal because it violated her commitment to ethical labour practices. At the time, it looked reckless—even self-sabotaging. Yet three years on, the business had scaled organically, retained its soul, and helped birth a new playbook for values-based investing. It's a reminder that decisions made from integrity don't always look impressive in the moment—but they often age remarkably well.

So, what does all this point to? That impact-driven decision-making is not some softer cousin of corporate strategy. It is its own rigorous, multidimensional practice—requiring sharper clarity, more complex trade-offs, and often, a thicker skin. It doesn't move fast. It doesn't always draw applause. But when it lands, it lands deeply—shaping not just ventures, but ecosystems.

In a culture fixated on speed and surface wins, the capacity to make thoughtful, values-aligned decisions is nothing short of subversive. It signals a departure from extractive models toward something regenerative. It suggests a founder who's not just building a business, but attempting to model a better way of being in the world.

And it all begins with a deceptively simple, endlessly difficult question: Does this move me closer to the world I'm trying to build?

If the answer is yes, proceed—even if the numbers waver. If no, pause—even if the opportunity gleams. Build the practices that let you return to that question, over and over, with greater confidence and deeper courage. Because in the end, legacy isn't shaped by how many decisions you made—but by the calibre of the ones you stood by when it mattered most.

The Values Compass: Making Choices Without Regret

In a world of infinite options and relentless demands, the ability to make decisions with clarity, consistency, and confidence is one of the most powerful assets a mission-driven entrepreneur can possess. But for those building businesses not only for profit but for purpose, decision-making is rarely straightforward. What seems logical on a spreadsheet may feel ethically ambiguous. What pleases investors may dilute the brand's deeper intention. What scales quickly may fracture the internal culture. In such high-stakes terrain, founders need more than strategic acumen—they need a compass. Not a moral abstraction, but a tangible framework for navigating choices that honours both the mission and the self. This is the essence of the *Values Compass*: a decision-making tool grounded in clarity, alignment, and the pursuit of outcomes that leave no residue of regret.

The concept of values-based decision-making is well supported in psychological literature. Researchers such as Dr Steven Hayes, founder of Acceptance and Commitment Therapy (ACT), have demonstrated that individuals who identify and act on their core values experience greater well-being, resilience, and long-term satisfaction—even in the face of stress or uncertainty. Similarly, organisational behaviour experts like Patrick Lencioni and Linda Treviño have found that companies anchored in values make more coherent decisions, attract more loyal stakeholders, and weather disruption with greater agility. The relevance of these insights to mission-driven ventures is profound. When your work is not merely commercial but ethical and cultural in nature, the cost of misaligned decisions is not just operational—it is existential.

The Values Compass provides a structured yet flexible way to engage with this complexity. At its foundation is the identification of non-negotiable principles: the handful of core beliefs that define the essence of your enterprise. These might include transparency, equity, sustainability, compassion, innovation, or dignity. The key is specificity. Broad platitudes are insufficient. "We care about people" means little until it is unpacked into measurable behaviours—how you hire, how you price, how you resolve conflict, how you scale. The more granular your values, the more useful they become as a decision filter.

Once identified, these values serve as anchoring coordinates. Every major decision—whether to raise investment, pivot the business model, enter a partnership, or hire a key leader—is tested against them. The question is no longer simply "What is possible?" or "What is profitable?" but "What is *right*—by our own standards?" This form of internal integrity is what philosopher Charles Taylor referred to as "strong evaluation": the ability to make choices based not just on desires or outcomes, but on qualitative distinctions about what is worth doing.

This framework is not theoretical. It has real-world application across industries. Consider Patagonia, the outdoor apparel company renowned for its environmental stewardship. When offered lucrative opportunities to expand into certain international markets, Patagonia declined—not because the markets weren't attractive, but because the required supply chain extensions would have violated their environmental standards. Their values compass told them that growing at the expense of ecological integrity was too high a price. As a result, their brand trust deepened, their team cohesion strengthened, and their long-term value increased.

Another compelling case is that of Sasha Dichter, former Chief Innovation Officer at Acumen, the global impact investment fund. At a critical juncture, Acumen was approached by a high-profile investor offering substantial capital with conditions that included changes to governance and strategy. On paper, it was a transformative deal. But the leadership team used a values-based decision framework to assess the proposal. When they asked, "Would accepting this capital require us to compromise on our founding belief in patient capital and stakeholder accountability?", the answer was yes. They walked away. The organisation not only preserved its integrity, but later secured funding from aligned partners on better terms.

These stories illustrate the power of values not as abstract ideals but as operational guides. They clarify the invisible costs of compromise and illuminate alternatives that might otherwise remain hidden. But they also reveal the courage required to follow the compass—especially when external voices push in other directions. One of the greatest challenges in values-based decision-making is dealing with the discomfort of disappointing others: investors who want faster growth, clients who demand concessions, team members who prefer shortcuts. The temptation to rationalise small deviations can be strong. But as behavioural economist Dan Ariely notes, "small dishonesty leads to larger dishonesty." Once the compass is abandoned, it becomes harder to locate again.

This is why the Values Compass is not only a personal tool but a cultural one. It must be socialised within the team, reinforced through storytelling, and encoded into systems. Organisations that integrate values into performance reviews, onboarding processes, and strategic planning are better able to institutionalise alignment. They create what management scholar Jim Collins calls "a cult-like culture"—not in the dogmatic sense, but in the consistency of shared commitments. When everyone is orienting to the same coordinates, decisions can be distributed without chaos, and accountability becomes a source of empowerment rather than surveillance.

Of course, not all values-based decisions are binary. Sometimes, tension exists *between* two cherished values—say, inclusivity and efficiency, or agility and transparency. In these moments, the compass must be used not to dictate answers, but to guide reflection. Which value is more core to our identity in this context? What will we sacrifice, and what are we preserving? These are not easy questions, but they are transformative ones. They move decision-making from transactional logic to moral imagination.

A striking example of this was seen during the early months of the COVID-19 pandemic. Many small businesses faced existential decisions about layoffs, closures, or pivots. Some rushed into survival mode, cutting costs indiscriminately. Others, like London-based social enterprise Brigade Bar & Kitchen, paused to reflect. They had always prioritised social reintegration for people affected by homelessness. Laying off staff would contradict that mission. Instead, they shifted operations to a community food delivery model, retained their most vulnerable team members, and partnered with local NGOs. Their revenue took a temporary hit, but their brand and team loyalty grew. Their decision, anchored in values, became a defining story of who they were.

The Values Compass also helps protect against one of the most corrosive forces in entrepreneurship: regret. Founders often make decisions under pressure, then second-guess them endlessly. This mental churn is costly—not just emotionally, but cognitively. A values-based framework offers a way to evaluate decisions not only by results, but by process. Even if a values-aligned choice leads to a setback, the founder can stand by it with peace. It was the right call *at the time*, given what was known and what mattered most. That peace—what philosopher Martha Nussbaum might call "moral stability"—is an often-overlooked but invaluable leadership resource.

In practice, the Values Compass is most powerful when used proactively, not reactively. When values are only invoked during crises, they become performative. But when used consistently—during strategic planning, during growth conversations, during hiring—it becomes muscle memory. Decision-making speeds up because direction is already known. Alignment is not something you chase; it's something you maintain.

To implement this, founders can begin with regular values reviews. Are our stated values still alive in our daily operations? Where are we drifting? What decisions lie ahead that may test our integrity? These questions, asked consistently, keep the compass calibrated. And over time, they turn value alignment from a theoretical aspiration into a lived, strategic advantage.

In a landscape saturated with options and influenced by trends, the ability to make grounded decisions is rare. The Values Compass offers not a formula, but a foundation—one that elevates clarity over cleverness, coherence over compromise. It is not always the easiest way to lead. But it is, more often than not, the wisest. And for those building businesses meant to last—not just in structure, but in soul—that wisdom is worth everything.

Opportunity Cost vs. True Cost: Rethinking Time, Money, and Energy

For decades, the calculus of return on investment (ROI) has been treated as a near-universal language in business strategy—an elegantly simple metric that claims to quantify the effectiveness of time and capital. Yet for founders operating at the intersection of purpose and profit, this framework is often reductive, if not outright misleading. The traditional model asks: *What do I gain for what I spend?* But in mission-driven enterprises, that gain is rarely just financial. And what's spent is not limited to money—it includes energy, trust, alignment, and even identity. This is where the concept of *true cost* becomes essential: a broader, more discerning lens that integrates both tangible and intangible dimensions into decision-making.

Understanding opportunity cost in its classical form is a starting point. Rooted in economic theory, it refers to the value of the next best alternative foregone when a decision is made. If you invest in marketing rather than product development, your opportunity cost is the potential return the product improvements might have delivered. This logic works well in zero-sum scenarios. But when applied without nuance to mission-led ventures, it risks distorting priorities. It undervalues intangibles, ignores long-term cultural impact, and favours measurable short-term outcomes over enduring systemic change.

The critical reframing, then, is to evolve from a narrow opportunity cost model to a *true cost* model—one that considers the full spectrum of inputs and outcomes. In this expanded model, cost is not merely what appears on an invoice. It's also what drains your team's energy, erodes your values, alienates your audience, or displaces your long-term vision. Likewise, returns are not limited to profit margins, but include increased stakeholder trust, community goodwill, personal satisfaction, and mission resilience.

Take the example of a social enterprise deciding whether to accept a high-paying consulting contract with a multinational corporation. The financial ROI is clear. But what is less immediately visible is the true cost: the time diverted from core activities, the stress placed on a small team, the reputational risks of alignment with a controversial brand, and the erosion of focus on the primary mission. If the project compromises internal morale, fragments attention, and delivers a product misaligned with the organisation's values, then the real return may be negative—even if the numbers suggest otherwise.

This misalignment becomes particularly evident when energy is treated as a renewable, costless input. In reality, energy is one of the most finite and fragile resources a mission-driven founder possesses. A decision that appears efficient on a spreadsheet may require disproportionate emotional labour, ethical compromise, or recovery time. If it leaves you creatively depleted or culturally off-kilter, its true cost must be reckoned with. Ignoring this dimension leads to what psychologist Adam Grant calls *empathy fatigue*—the slow erosion of the capacity to care, often masked by outward success.

Traditional ROI frameworks also struggle with what economists refer to as *externalities*—costs or benefits that affect third parties but are not reflected in market prices. In social impact work, externalities are everywhere. A decision to outsource manufacturing might reduce costs in the short term but degrade working conditions, increase carbon emissions, or weaken local economic ecosystems. These costs, though not captured in immediate P&L statements, are real—and increasingly visible to consumers, employees, and investors.

Modern mission-led brands are beginning to integrate this thinking into their operating models. Consider the example of Allbirds, a sustainable footwear company that has redefined industry metrics by incorporating carbon cost into every product decision. Rather than optimising for profit alone, the company calculates the environmental footprint of each shoe and uses that data as part of its internal decision-making matrix. Their leadership explicitly states that products must "perform for the planet" as well as the business. This mindset reframes opportunity cost entirely: the cost of using a cheaper material isn't just a missed margin—it's an increased ecological burden, a reputational liability, and a breach of brand trust.

True cost thinking also influences the internal tempo of a business. One of the least discussed opportunity costs in entrepreneurship is the cost of *doing too much.* Pursuing multiple initiatives simultaneously may feel productive but often leads to diluted focus, inconsistent execution, and staff burnout. Each "yes" carries an invisible cost: every new project competes with existing ones for energy, attention, and clarity. In contrast, saying "no" to a tempting opportunity is not always a loss—it can be a strategic preservation of momentum, coherence, and sanity.

This principle played out visibly in the case of Basecamp, the project management software company. Rather than scaling aggressively or pursuing venture capital, the founders intentionally capped growth and restricted product sprawl. Their rationale? Each expansion carried a cost—not just in terms of infrastructure, but in the clarity of the product and the culture of the team. By privileging focus over scale, they avoided the true cost of overextension: a bloated product, a burned-out team, and a drift from their founding values. The decision defied conventional metrics but proved prescient in its long-term sustainability.

To integrate true cost thinking into practice, leaders must cultivate what Harvard Business School professor Rosabeth Moss Kanter calls *kaleidoscope thinking*—the ability to see a situation from multiple angles, beyond the obvious. This requires slowing down the decision-making process enough to ask better questions. What are we not seeing in this data? Who else is affected by this choice? What emotional or reputational energy will this consume? How will this decision feel six months from now—not just to us, but to our stakeholders?

These questions demand a kind of psychological spaciousness that is often at odds with the pressure to act fast. Yet it is precisely in this space that better decisions emerge—decisions that balance boldness with foresight, and strategy with empathy. This is not about being risk-averse. It is about being *risk-intelligent*—understanding that the most dangerous risks are often those we do not name because they don't fit neatly into a spreadsheet.

Even time itself—the ultimate constraint—is subject to revaluation under this model. Entrepreneurs are taught to view time as a cost, to be minimised or "hacked." But when time is spent deepening relationships, nourishing team culture, or refining a product to align more fully with purpose, it is not a cost. It is an investment. A longer launch timeline might appear inefficient in quarterly reporting, but if it leads to a stronger brand, a more resilient team, or fewer ethical missteps, its true ROI is often far greater.

The most transformative aspect of true cost thinking is that it restores a sense of moral agency to business. It invites leaders to move beyond narrow optimisation and toward holistic stewardship. To weigh decisions not only by how they affect the bottom line, but by how they shape the world—and the self. In doing so, it elevates entrepreneurship from technical execution to ethical leadership.

For founders building mission-aligned ventures, this approach is not optional—it is necessary. The stakes of your work are too high, the complexity too great, to rely solely on traditional ROI metrics. The true cost of a decision includes what it demands of your team, your conscience, your clarity. And the true return includes what it allows you to sleep with at night, what it enables you to build five years from now, and who it helps you become in the process.

Rethinking cost in this way is not merely a financial shift. It is a philosophical one. It is the recognition that your time, your energy, and your integrity are non-renewable assets—and that any decision that sacrifices them without adequate return is too expensive, no matter how profitable it looks on paper.

To lead with impact, you must learn to see with both microscope and telescope. To weigh the numbers, but also the narrative. To ask, always: *What will this truly cost us—and what are we truly gaining?* The answers may not be simple, but they will be honest. And that honesty, sustained over time, is what turns good intentions into enduring, regenerative change.

The Eisenhower Matrix for Mission-Driven Entrepreneurs

In the ever-expanding landscape of entrepreneurship, especially for those leading mission-driven ventures, time is not merely a resource—it is a crucible. Every hour demands decisions not just about tasks, but about values. Unlike traditional founders, who might prioritise market share, revenue velocity, or operational scale, impact-driven entrepreneurs are often working at the confluence of ethics, service, and sustainability. This complexity can quickly lead to overload, not because the leader lacks focus, but because *everything feels important.* In such contexts, the classic Eisenhower Matrix—a productivity tool born from military precision—can be repurposed and recalibrated to meet the nuanced needs of purpose-led leadership.

Originally attributed to Dwight D. Eisenhower, the 34th President of the United States and Supreme Commander of the Allied Forces during World War II, the matrix was designed to help leaders prioritise effectively under intense pressure. It classifies tasks into four quadrants based on urgency and importance: urgent and important, important but not urgent, urgent but not important, and neither urgent nor important. While this framework has stood the test of time, its application in mission-driven contexts requires a fundamental shift—not just in what we label as urgent or important, but in how we *define* those terms in the first place.

For entrepreneurs guided by impact, the traditional emphasis on speed, deadlines, and deliverables often clashes with the slower, deeper rhythms of systemic change. A campaign launch may feel urgent, but is it *important* in advancing the mission's core objectives? A speaking invitation may carry visibility, but does it serve long-term strategic integrity? These questions highlight the need to adapt the matrix—not by discarding it, but by enriching it with context, values, and emotional intelligence.

The first adaptation is rethinking *urgency*. In conventional frameworks, urgency is determined by time-sensitivity—tasks that are deadline-driven or consequence-laden. But in mission-driven work, urgency also carries a moral dimension. An environmental crisis, a sudden shift in community needs, or an unexpected social media storm may demand immediate response—not because it affects quarterly results, but because silence would betray the mission. Thus, urgency for the impact entrepreneur includes *ethical immediacy*, not just operational timelines.

This redefinition allows the "urgent and important" quadrant to be populated more thoughtfully. These are not just firefighting tasks, but mission-critical moments—those inflection points that require fast, values-aligned decisions. The COVID-19 pandemic provided countless such examples. Purpose-led businesses had to decide quickly how to protect staff, support customers, and remain useful in a rapidly evolving crisis. Those who had already built decision-making around values—such as social enterprise networks like B Lab—were able to act swiftly without losing coherence. Their version of the Eisenhower Matrix included a real-time assessment of social responsibility, not just internal continuity.

The second adaptation concerns *importance.* In traditional usage, importance is tied to long-term goals and high-stakes outcomes. For the mission-driven leader, importance must be linked to *impact alignment.* It is not enough for a task to generate visibility, revenue, or engagement. It must advance the mission in a meaningful, measurable way. This requires more than intuition—it demands clarity around organisational objectives, stakeholder needs, and value metrics.

Consider the example of Rubicon, a social enterprise focused on ending waste through technology. When evaluating strategic partnerships, CEO Nate Morris applies a rigorously values-driven filter. A proposal may appear commercially attractive, but if it doesn't align with the company's environmental mission or complicates its transparency commitments, it's deprioritised. This discipline in identifying what is *truly important*—even when tempting opportunities arise—is the hallmark of strategic maturity. It's the difference between growing and growing well.

In the adapted matrix, the "important but not urgent" quadrant takes on heightened significance. This is the space where vision lives—where the slow, often invisible work of culture-building, strategy development, stakeholder engagement, and leadership reflection occurs. In traditional entrepreneurial cultures, these activities are often postponed in favour of tasks with immediate output. But for mission-driven enterprises, this quadrant is sacred. It is where depth is cultivated, where ethical clarity is sharpened, and where the foundations for long-term resilience are laid.

Neglecting this quadrant leads to strategic drift. When mission-led entrepreneurs get caught in reactive cycles—constantly responding to external demands—they lose the capacity to think, design, and evolve. The irony is that many leaders know these tasks are important, but they defer them because they lack urgency. The adapted matrix demands a different discipline: scheduling what is valuable even when it is not visible. Making time for internal alignment, team debriefs, values clarification, and stakeholder listening is not ancillary—it is the work.

The third quadrant—urgent but not important—presents one of the greatest threats to impact-driven leadership. These are tasks that scream for attention but deliver little lasting value: minor logistical issues, performative gestures, vanity metrics, reactive PR. In a digital age obsessed with constant visibility, this quadrant grows by the day. Mission-driven founders are particularly vulnerable here, as they are often pulled in by guilt or the desire to please. A quick call, a panel appearance, a last-minute funding proposal that doesn't truly fit—each may feel too small to decline, but together they siphon energy, dilute focus, and crowd out the space needed for real work.

The adapted Eisenhower Matrix demands that entrepreneurs *interrogate urgency*. Why does this feel pressing? Who defines the timeline? What would happen if we said no? By reclaiming control over what is responded to—and what is not—leaders create space for authenticity. They also build organisational cultures that value discernment over busyness. Teams that see their leaders protecting strategic priorities are more likely to focus on meaningful execution rather than reactive activity.

Finally, the fourth quadrant—neither urgent nor important—is less common in the intense ecosystem of social impact, but it still surfaces. Endless email threads, shallow networking events, ceremonial meetings. These are the low-grade distractors that offer a brief sense of activity but deliver no progress. In mission-led ventures, these tasks are often inherited through inertia or institutional habit. The discipline here is not just individual, but structural: removing or redesigning low-value rituals, streamlining processes, and fostering a culture that questions inherited practices. What worked for a traditional business may not serve a values-based enterprise.

To bring this adaptation to life, some entrepreneurs have created visual boards of their mission-aligned Eisenhower Matrix—replacing traditional labels with ones such as "Respond with integrity," "Design with purpose," "Delay with clarity," and

"Eliminate with compassion." These reminders help translate abstract concepts into daily action, anchoring the team's rhythm in shared priorities.

The matrix also works as a reflective tool. At the end of each week or quarter, reviewing how time was spent across the quadrants can reveal unconscious biases. Was too much time spent reacting? Were the most important tasks deprioritised? Did we attend to our values or simply manage tasks? These questions invite honest course correction and re-alignment.

Ultimately, the adapted Eisenhower Matrix is not merely a productivity tool—it is a lens for ethical entrepreneurship. It honours the complexity of purpose-led leadership without collapsing it into vague aspiration. It offers a framework for making real-time decisions that protect long-term purpose. And most importantly, it reminds leaders that urgency and importance are not objective facts, but subjective judgments—judgments that must be rooted not in fear, popularity, or speed, but in clarity, integrity, and courage.

For the mission-driven entrepreneur, this version of the matrix becomes more than a quadrant on paper. It becomes a daily practice—a compass for navigating the chaos with conviction. Because in a world that values more, faster, louder, the quiet clarity of purposeful prioritisation is not only radical. It is indispensable.

Gut Feeling vs. Data-Driven Strategy: When to Trust Instincts in Business

Few dilemmas challenge entrepreneurs more consistently than the choice between intuition and analytics. The modern business landscape is saturated with data—metrics, dashboards, heatmaps, and projections—all purporting to guide strategic action. At the same time, founders and leaders frequently speak of moments when they "just knew" what decision to make. This apparent paradox—between gut feeling and empirical evidence—raises a profound question: when should a decision-maker trust their instincts, and when must they defer to the data?

For mission-driven entrepreneurs, the question is not merely tactical. It touches the core of what makes their work distinct. Their enterprises are not built solely on profit maximisation or market penetration. They are expressions of values, vision, and often deeply personal convictions. This intertwining of identity and enterprise intensifies the role of intuition, while simultaneously increasing the stakes of getting a decision wrong.

To engage with this tension meaningfully, we must begin by demystifying intuition itself. Contrary to popular belief, gut feeling is not a mystical sixth sense. Cognitive science defines intuition as the brain's ability to make rapid, unconscious assessments based on accumulated experience and pattern recognition. Nobel laureate Daniel Kahneman, in his seminal work *Thinking, Fast and Slow*, distinguishes between System 1 (intuitive, automatic) and System 2 (analytical, deliberate) thinking. Intuition, or System 1, is faster and more emotionally charged, while analytical reasoning, or System 2, is slower but more rigorous.

Kahneman warns, however, that intuition can be dangerously flawed—prone to bias, overconfidence, and snap judgments. Yet he also acknowledges that in specific domains—particularly where feedback is consistent and patterns are recognisable—experts can develop remarkably reliable instincts. This distinction is critical. Intuition becomes trustworthy when it is *earned* through deep immersion and honed across many cycles of trial, error, and reflection.

In the context of entrepreneurship, seasoned founders often rely on pattern recognition in product development, team dynamics, or market timing. A social entrepreneur who has spent years embedded in a particular community may pick up on subtle shifts—emotional undercurrents, cultural cues, behavioural inflections—that no dataset could quantify. Their "gut" is not irrational; it is data-rich, albeit tacit. The danger emerges when intuition operates outside its domain of validity—when a leader uses personal instinct to navigate unfamiliar terrain, misinterprets weak signals, or confuses wishful thinking with insight.

This is where data comes in—not as a replacement for intuition, but as its complement and counterbalance. In environments of complexity and uncertainty, data can reveal patterns too subtle for human perception, challenge entrenched assumptions, and provide the evidentiary scaffolding for high-stakes decisions. But even data is not immune to distortion. It can be incomplete, outdated, biased in collection or interpretation. It can be used to reinforce existing beliefs rather than challenge them. And it often lacks the nuance to capture the full texture of human behaviour, especially in mission-led contexts where success is measured in more than metrics.

The key, then, is *integration.* The most effective leaders do not polarise instinct and evidence—they synthesise them. They know when to test their gut against data, and when to interrogate the limitations of the data through lived experience. This skill—what some scholars call "sensemaking"—is less about choosing one mode over the other and more about knowing which to privilege in a given context.

Consider the case of Anne Wojcicki, co-founder of the genetic testing company 23andMe. In the company's early days, many investors were sceptical about the viability of offering consumers direct access to their genetic data. The market data was inconclusive, and the regulatory environment was opaque. But Wojcicki had a strong instinct—drawn from her background in healthcare and her conviction about consumer empowerment—that people were ready to engage with their genetic health. Her gut told her this was a cultural moment, not just a business opportunity. That instinct, tempered by careful scenario analysis and feedback from early adopters, led to a bold strategy that positioned 23andMe as a pioneer in personalised medicine. She trusted her gut—but she didn't abandon the numbers. She used them to refine, not define, the vision.

A contrasting example is provided by the cautionary tale of Quibi, the short-form streaming platform that raised nearly $2 billion before collapsing within six months of launch. Founded by seasoned executives Jeffrey Katzenberg and Meg Whitman, Quibi was driven more by conviction than evidence. Despite early warnings from consumer testing and digital behaviour data—

suggesting users were not ready to pay for bite-sized content on mobile—the founders pushed ahead. Their instincts, forged in traditional media, did not translate well to the rapidly evolving tech ecosystem. In this case, intuition ignored data, and the result was a spectacular failure.

For mission-driven founders, the stakes of this balance are particularly acute. Their decisions often involve trade-offs not just between growth and cost, but between competing values—access versus quality, speed versus equity, innovation versus inclusion. These decisions rarely yield clear data-driven answers. In such cases, intuition becomes not a shortcut, but a container for complexity. It allows leaders to feel into decisions that numbers cannot fully resolve. But it must be tested, made explicit, and refined through dialogue and feedback.

Practical applications of this integrated approach are already emerging in sectors like human-centred design and behavioural economics. Design thinking, for instance, encourages iterative prototyping—testing intuitive ideas quickly and refining them through data collected in real-world use. This protects vision while embracing learning. Behavioural economics, on the other hand, offers tools to recognise and mitigate cognitive biases that often distort both gut and data interpretation—such as confirmation bias, availability bias, and sunk cost fallacy.

Mission-led enterprises would do well to incorporate such disciplines into their strategic processes. One useful exercise is the "pre-mortem"—a thought experiment in which a team imagines that a project has failed and works backward to identify why. This engages both intuitive foresight and analytical risk assessment. Another technique is triangulation: testing a decision through multiple lenses—quantitative analysis, stakeholder feedback, and values alignment. The more a decision holds up across diverse inputs, the more robust it becomes.

The future of leadership will likely reward those who cultivate this dual fluency—the capacity to move fluidly between data and instinct, reason and feeling, precision and presence. It is no longer enough to be numerate or visionary alone. The complexity of today's challenges demands that leaders learn to hold paradox: to act decisively while staying curious, to trust their gut while checking their bias, to believe in their mission while adapting their model.

At its best, the tension between intuition and data is not a battleground but a crucible—a place where better decisions are forged. It invites humility, rigour, and continuous learning. And it reminds us that entrepreneurship is not a science or an art, but an *ethic*—a way of making choices that honour both the realities of the world and the responsibilities of one's purpose.

For the impact-driven entrepreneur, the question is never simply, "What does the data say?" or "What does my gut say?" It is: *What do they say together?* And more importantly: *How can I design my decisions so that both my intuition and my analysis make each other wiser?*

To lead in this way is not to possess perfect judgment, but to pursue wise action. And in the uncertain, high-stakes realm of mission-led ventures, that pursuit—when grounded in both instinct and evidence—is perhaps the most powerful strategy of all.

Case Study: A Social Entrepreneur's Risky Bet That Changed an Industry

In the world of social entrepreneurship, risk is not just financial—it is philosophical. When a leader chooses to align their business around a cause rather than a conventional growth metric, every decision becomes an act of value signalling, not merely market signalling. Nowhere is this more evident than in the case of Tolu Olubunmi, the founder of *Impact Without Borders*, whose high-stakes decision to restructure her mission-led organisation disrupted prevailing norms in the education-to-employment pipeline—and in doing so, created a ripple effect that challenged systemic assumptions across multiple sectors.

Olubunmi, an engineer by training and an undocumented immigrant by circumstance, entered the social enterprise world not through business school but through advocacy. After years of working in Washington on immigration reform and youth policy, she grew frustrated with the limitations of nonprofit advocacy in creating structural employment access for marginalised communities. Her insight was deceptively simple: what young talent lacked was not merely opportunity, but *infrastructure*—pathways that translated potential into tangible, dignified employment.

With this insight, Olubunmi launched *Impact Without Borders* as a hybrid organisation, initially structured as a nonprofit with a services arm. The goal was to bridge the divide between untapped talent—particularly immigrant, refugee, and undocumented youth—and the innovation economy. Early traction came from partnering with community colleges and local workforce agencies to offer digital skills boot camps, paired with mentorship and career coaching. The impact was clear. Retention rates were high. Job placements outperformed traditional programmes. Donor funding flowed steadily.

But within two years, she faced a dilemma familiar to many social entrepreneurs: how to scale a mission without diluting it. Her nonprofit status constrained the ability to innovate with productised offerings. Revenue was project-based, vulnerable to funder cycles. Meanwhile, demand from tech firms seeking diverse, purpose-aligned talent was growing exponentially. Consultants advised her to remain within the nonprofit ecosystem and pursue government contracts. Others pushed for a traditional pivot—venture capital, Silicon Valley advisors, standardised curricula. Yet Olubunmi sensed that neither path fit the soul of her work.

It was at this juncture that she made her risky bet: to convert *Impact Without Borders* into a public benefit corporation (PBC), shut down the nonprofit entity entirely, and build a proprietary talent-matching platform that would operate on a tiered subscription model for employers, while remaining free for learners. This decision alienated some funders, confused policy allies, and raised eyebrows among peers. Why dismantle a proven nonprofit? Why commercialise access for marginalised groups? Why trust that mission integrity would survive the transition?

Her answer was clear: *because sustainability without sovereignty was no longer acceptable.* For Olubunmi, mission alignment meant more than being values-driven. It meant building an entity whose business model *embodied* the change it sought. Relying on charitable capital to solve economic exclusion felt increasingly contradictory. The bet, she argued, was not on markets over values—but on values shaping markets.

Critics questioned whether her target population would be served better through philanthropic models. The platform, they worried, could slide into the logic of conventional hiring marketplaces—efficiency over empathy. But Olubunmi's design choices reflected deep intentionality. The algorithm wasn't built on résumé keywords, but on competency-based assessments, peer feedback, and contextual interviews that surfaced non-traditional experience. Employer partners were required to complete unconscious bias training and adhere to inclusive hiring metrics. Revenue was reinvested into coaching and upskilling cohorts that had been most systemically marginalised—Black immigrants, DACA recipients, and forcibly displaced youth.

Over time, the results spoke louder than the scepticism. Within three years of relaunch, *Impact Without Borders* had facilitated over 5,000 job placements across four continents. Median salaries for participants increased by 70%, with a retention rate 40% higher than industry norms. More remarkably, several employer partners reported cultural transformation within their teams—less attrition, greater engagement, and more inclusive leadership development. The platform had not just matched people to jobs—it had challenged the very architecture of hiring.

What made Olubunmi's bet transformative was not just the outcome, but the *process*. She reimagined risk not as a function of deviation from convention, but as fidelity to purpose. Her bold move challenged two assumptions: first, that mission and money exist in opposition; and second, that scale must always follow a template. By refusing both binary thinking and incrementalism, she carved out a third way—an enterprise that scaled not despite its values, but *because* of them.

The theoretical underpinnings of her approach find resonance in the concept of *transformative resilience*, a term used in organisational psychology to describe systems that don't just bounce back from disruption but use it as a catalyst for evolution. Olubunmi leaned into disruption not as an obstacle but as a crucible. Her reconfiguration of the enterprise model exemplified a form of adaptive leadership where long-term mission integrity outweighed short-term consensus.

There are key lessons here for other mission-led entrepreneurs navigating the tension between authenticity and adaptation. First, clarity of purpose is non-negotiable. Olubunmi's decision was not a reaction to market trends; it was a response to deep alignment. Second, mission is a design principle, not just a message. The choices embedded in product architecture, user experience, pricing, and partnership terms are where values are either operationalised or abandoned. Third, risk is reframed when impact becomes the core ROI. Olubunmi was willing to trade familiarity for flexibility because she believed that only structural ownership—not programme dependency—would create enduring change.

The broader implications of this case reach beyond employment or education. They challenge all sectors to reconsider what "success" means in the impact economy. When conventional metrics—scale, speed, capital raised—are decoupled from mission, enterprises risk becoming hollow vessels. But when mission is embedded not only in intent but in infrastructure, even radical pivots become coherent.

Today, *Impact Without Borders* is not merely a platform. It is a proof point—a living counterargument to the idea that social justice must wait until after profitability. It reminds us that the boldest decisions often emerge not from spreadsheets, but from conviction. And that the entrepreneurs most likely to change industries are not those who hedge their bets, but those who wager everything on alignment.

Olubunmi's story, in its full complexity, demonstrates that defying convention is not recklessness when it is grounded in rigorous reflection, community accountability, and systemic insight. Her risky bet worked not because it avoided trade-offs, but because it made them visible—and then honoured them. For anyone seeking to lead a business that doesn't just survive but transforms, the message is clear: the riskiest move is often not the one that breaks with tradition, but the one that breaks with purpose.

And when mission leads, the market often follows. Eventually.

Chapter 6
Building a Financially Resilient Mission

Financial resilience isn't some luxury reserved for later; for the mission-driven entrepreneur, it's the spine of the operation. Without it, even the most inspiring purpose becomes fragile—at the mercy of funding gaps, burnout, or decisions made in desperation. Yet, curiously, in the world of social impact, money often lingers on the margins of conversation. It's treated as a necessary evil, a quiet background concern rather than a central design principle. This chapter sets out to change that dynamic. Running a resilient, values-led venture doesn't mean putting profit above purpose—but it does mean understanding that vision, no matter how compelling, won't pay the bills. Without financial literacy, thoughtful planning, and a structure built to withstand more than a fair-weather forecast, impact cannot scale—and may not survive.

This discomfort with money in mission-focused circles isn't unfounded. Many founders arrive at this work not from the world of finance, but from activism, advocacy, or service. Their instincts point toward justice, not revenue generation. And that's a strength—but it can become a liability if left untempered by strategy. The most enduring changemakers aren't those who ignore money, but those who bring it into the same ethical frame as their purpose. They don't see cash flow as antithetical to conscience. On the contrary, they understand that funding mechanisms, far from being neutral, shape outcomes just as much as any theory of change.

So where to begin? At the basics, frankly. And not the kind of basics that get a quick glance and are left to someone else on the team. Budgeting, cash flow forecasting, pricing strategies—these aren't just operational tasks; they are strategic acts. Know the difference between restricted and unrestricted income, between fixed and variable costs, and you're better positioned to absorb the next funding delay or policy shift. The world doesn't run on best-case scenarios. Enterprises grounded in mission must be built for volatility. That means designing lean, planning for surprises, and weaving transparency into every financial thread.

Still, while stability is important, it's hardly the whole story. Resilience asks more. It asks for resourcefulness. Because traditional funding flows—particularly the fast, risk-tolerant capital—often favour ventures chasing scale over those rooted in impact. For mission-led founders, this requires a more nuanced approach. Grants, catalytic capital, equity with long-term horizons, revenue-based financing—each comes with its own expectations and its own consequences. And not all impact investors are cut from the same cloth. Some prioritise storytelling over sustainability. Others want mission adherence, but only so long as the growth curve stays steep. Founders must learn to read the fine print—not just legally, but culturally.

The story of All We Are offers a case in point. Initially driven by grant funding to deliver solar infrastructure in Uganda, the organisation soon hit a wall—demand outpaced what donor capital could support. So, founder Nathan Thomas reimagined the structure: creating a for-profit arm to attract investment, while preserving nonprofit oversight on quality and impact. A delicate manoeuvre, but one that paid off. It wasn't just financially savvy—it was a principled evolution. The organisation didn't dilute its mission; it reinforced it by diversifying how it was funded.

At the core of this shift is a concept gaining traction: profit for purpose. It's a tricky phrase—easily misunderstood, often misused. But when executed with precision, it becomes a powerful model. Businesses like Nisolo, Veja, Kiva, and M-KOPA have shown that market mechanisms can support, rather than distort, social objectives. But it requires care. Revenue generation must be more than a survival tactic—it must be intentionally engineered to further the mission. It's not enough to make money and then do good. The doing of good must be embedded in the very act of making money.

This is why the term "business model" shouldn't be relegated to investor decks. It should sit alongside mission statements and impact metrics. A resilient model isn't built on assumptions—it's forged through iteration, evidence, and feedback. Underpricing, for example, may seem noble—a way to remain accessible or humble—but it can backfire. It sends signals of undervaluation, fosters reliance on subsidies, and, over time, starves the organisation of the energy and resources it needs to thrive. Pricing, in this sense, isn't just about numbers. It's about self-respect, sustainability, and limits.

Of course, all of this is complicated by the money stories many founders carry. These are rarely spoken aloud, but they shape behaviour nonetheless. Some believe it's somehow unprincipled to turn a profit. Others equate fundraising with manipulation. Still others see wealth and ethics as mutually exclusive domains. These beliefs—deep-seated and often inherited—are corrosive. They keep leaders in cycles of scarcity, stretching themselves thin in the name of virtue. But here's the truth: money is not inherently corrupting. Like any tool, its value depends on how—and why—it is used. Aligned with purpose, it becomes not a compromise, but a catalyst.

This internal shift must translate into practice. Which is why this chapter culminates in a hands-on framework: the Personal Financial Roadmap for Impact. Less a spreadsheet and more a compass, this tool encourages founders to get brutally honest about their own needs and the needs of their venture. Not just what's required to scrape by—but what's necessary to sustain energy, support a team, and hold space for long-term ambition. The roadmap then moves outward: How might revenue streams be diversified in ways that serve, rather than strain, the mission? What kind of capital best supports the soul of the work?

Then comes perhaps the most neglected aspect: rhythm. Financial planning isn't a one-off activity. It's a practice. Too many impact leaders sprint after scale, forgetting to breathe. The roadmap introduces pacing tools—signposts for when to invest, when to pause, when to stretch, and when to consolidate. In a sector that often rewards hustle and self-sacrifice, these signals help shift the focus from urgency to coherence. And coherence—when vision, operations, and money speak the same language—is what truly fortifies a venture.

It's in this alignment that something powerful happens. Investors stop feeling like interrogators and start behaving like allies. Revenue no longer triggers guilt, but pride. The organisation becomes supple, responsive—able not just to weather change, but to influence it. And that, in the end, is the kind of enterprise the impact economy needs.

As this ecosystem grows, one distinction will become more important than ever: the difference between fragile idealism and grounded, resilient pragmatism. The latter doesn't abandon values—it honours them with structure. This kind of resilience isn't glamorous. You won't see it featured in glossy campaigns or lauded on keynote stages. But it is the hidden architecture of sustainable impact. It's the frame that holds the vision upright, even when conditions shake.

So here is the invitation: step into that architecture willingly. Let money be part of the mission—not a detour from it. Understand that sustainability isn't a buzzword; it's a promise. One that says: this work matters enough to last. When founders build financial models that reflect their values, when they stop apologising for needing resources, when they design not for perfection but for coherence—that's when impact becomes truly transformational. Not just an idea, but a force. Powered by purpose. Sustained by strategy. And capable, finally, of reshaping the world it seeks to serve.

The Financial Foundations of a Mission-Led Life

In the mission-driven world, passion and purpose often take centre stage—rightly so. Entrepreneurs who commit to addressing society's most pressing problems bring unmatched dedication and vision. Yet, for all their clarity of purpose, many impact-focused leaders falter on a critical front: money management. The discomfort is understandable. Traditional models of finance are laden with extractive logics and short-term thinking, elements often antithetical to ethical entrepreneurship. But to sidestep financial literacy in the name of integrity is not noble—it's self-sabotaging. The truth is simple but non-negotiable: if your mission matters, it must be financially viable. And financial viability begins with personal and organisational mastery of foundational money management skills.

This is not about becoming a finance expert or betraying your ideals. It's about reclaiming financial agency as part of the architecture of sustainable impact. Without a healthy relationship with money, even the most compelling mission will struggle to survive, let alone scale. Managing money well is not a distraction from purpose—it's a vital expression of it.

The starting point is to reframe finance not as a technical burden, but as a strategic language. Money tells a story. It reveals what we value, where we focus, and how we translate ideals into action. When founders begin to read their bank statements not just for numbers but for patterns—patterns in spending, risk tolerance, and investment—they begin to uncover deep insights into their leadership psychology. Are resources being funnelled toward growth or maintenance? Are they funding urgency or impact? Are personal finances propping up an unsustainable business model?

This lens is especially critical in early-stage enterprises, where the boundary between personal and organisational money is often blurred. Many founders bootstrap their ventures with personal savings, loans, or income from side work. While admirable, this blend requires precision. Without clear demarcation, founders risk not only tax complications but emotional exhaustion. Personal financial clarity—knowing your monthly needs, setting income goals, maintaining reserves—is essential to avoid martyrdom. A mission-led life must include a sustainable livelihood for its leader.

An instructive example comes from Leah Lizarondo, co-founder of Food Rescue Hero, a tech platform connecting surplus food to those in need. In the organisation's infancy, Lizarondo supported the work through freelance consulting while carefully managing her living costs. She set a target for when she would transition to full-time leadership and treated her finances as a runway, not a sacrifice. This deliberate approach allowed her to scale the organisation responsibly, avoid burnout, and model financial self-respect for her team. Her experience underscores that managing money well is not about greed—it's about endurance.

Budgeting, though mundane in reputation, is another core skill often underestimated by mission-driven entrepreneurs. A values-aligned budget is not simply a list of expenses; it is a reflection of strategic priorities. Allocating funds is a form of decision-making. Are you investing in marketing because visibility drives impact, or because of fear of irrelevance? Are you underinvesting in staff development due to scarcity thinking, or are there genuinely better returns elsewhere? These are not spreadsheet questions—they are leadership questions.

Effective budgeting also helps founders confront the real cost of their mission. Many underestimate what it takes to deliver their offering at a high standard—underpricing services, over-relying on unpaid labour, or postponing infrastructure investments. This creates a chronic fragility, a state of constant scrambling. Budgeting with integrity means costing your vision properly and charging appropriately, even if it challenges internalised narratives about what purpose should "look like."

Cash flow management, closely tied to budgeting, often marks the line between survival and shutdown. Impact ventures are particularly vulnerable to cash flow volatility due to seasonal grants, delayed client payments, or irregular revenue cycles. Founders must learn to track inflows and outflows with regularity—not to become obsessed with liquidity, but to remain alert to signs of stress. Cash flow forecasting, even in simple forms, enables smarter decisions around hiring, procurement, and growth timing. It builds a buffer against crisis, not unlike emotional regulation in a high-stakes conversation.

One overlooked but transformative practice is *reserves planning*. Too many social enterprises live grant-to-grant or contract-to-contract, leaving no margin for adaptation. Building financial reserves—however modest—sends a signal: we are designing for resilience, not dependence. It also creates strategic breathing room. With reserves, leaders can experiment, weather disruptions, or make values-aligned decisions without being coerced by cash constraints.

Debt is another area where nuance matters. Mission-driven founders often shy away from borrowing, associating it with risk or compromise. But debt, when used strategically, can be a tool for empowerment. A low-interest loan to upgrade technology, expand capacity, or bridge a funding gap is not inherently irresponsible. What matters is the repayment plan, the alignment with business goals, and the clarity of terms. Founders should ask: is this debt increasing our capacity to deliver impact—or merely compensating for poor planning?

To navigate these complexities, entrepreneurs must build financial fluency—not just for themselves, but within their teams. When mission-aligned organisations avoid financial transparency, they disempower staff, erode trust, and miss opportunities for collective wisdom. Inclusive financial practices—such as open-book management or participatory budgeting—allow staff to see how money flows, how trade-offs are made, and how their work connects to organisational sustainability. This fosters a culture where money is discussed without fear, not as a taboo but as a shared responsibility.

Beyond technical proficiency, the psychological dimension of money must be addressed. Many impact leaders carry unresolved narratives around wealth, scarcity, and worthiness. They may feel guilt around charging for services, discomfort receiving salaries, or anxiety discussing financial performance. These patterns often stem from early life experiences, cultural conditioning, or activist environments where money was equated with corruption. To lead financially resilient lives, founders must rewrite these scripts. Money, in itself, is neither virtuous nor corrupt—it is neutral. What gives it moral weight is how it is earned, used, and distributed.

Take the example of Sara Blakely, the founder of Spanx, who built her billion-dollar brand with a deep commitment to women's empowerment. Though not operating in a traditionally "mission-driven" industry, she structured her finances and company culture to reflect her values—giving equity to employees, donating millions to support female entrepreneurs, and ensuring the financial model supported both profit and purpose. Her story shows that a values-led financial life is not constrained to nonprofits or impact niches—it is a mindset available to anyone willing to align money with meaning.

To operationalise this alignment, purpose-led entrepreneurs benefit from creating a *personal finance dashboard*—a living document that includes income goals, savings targets, impact investments, and giving plans. It serves as a mirror, reflecting not only where your money goes but whether it aligns with your declared values. Over time, this dashboard becomes a compass, helping founders make decisions not just efficiently but *ethically*.

Ultimately, financial foundations are not about accumulating wealth—they are about building capacity. The capacity to respond to opportunities without desperation. The capacity to protect your team, uphold your values, and grow your impact without losing sleep or compromising your mission. They are what allow a vision to move from aspiration to execution—and then from execution to scale.

A mission-led life that ignores money is not idealistic. It is incomplete. Financial mastery, when rooted in self-awareness and purpose, becomes a form of activism. It models a new way of doing business—one that is not extractive, but generative. Not exploitative, but equitable. And not reactive, but regenerative.

This is the invitation: not to become obsessed with money, but to become fluent in it. To wield it with clarity, courage, and conscience. Because the future of ethical enterprise does not belong to those who fear finance, but to those who master it in service of something greater. Financial health is not the opposite of mission. It is what makes mission possible.

Funding Your Mission: Grants, Investors, and Creative Financing

Securing capital for a mission-driven venture requires more than a compelling vision—it demands a financing strategy as intentional, values-aligned, and resilient as the mission itself. While traditional startups often pursue a singular route—venture capital or bootstrapping—purpose-led businesses must navigate a more intricate ecosystem, balancing financial sustainability with ethical coherence. The task is not simply to raise funds, but to *curate capital* that amplifies rather than dilutes the enterprise's impact. This chapter explores the diverse funding pathways available to mission-driven founders, the nuances of ethical investment, and the creative tools being used by social entrepreneurs to finance change without compromising their values.

At the heart of this discussion is a paradigm shift: away from extractive capital models and toward regenerative finance. In conventional funding logic, investors seek outsized returns, often on accelerated timelines, with limited regard for social or environmental consequences. This pressure can force founders to scale prematurely, cut corners on integrity, or pivot away from the communities they originally sought to serve. Mission-aligned funding rejects this zero-sum mentality. It recognises that profit and purpose can—and must—coexist, but only if the financial architecture is deliberately designed to support that balance.

Grants, traditionally associated with the nonprofit sector, remain a critical and often underutilised source of capital for social enterprises. Philanthropic funders are increasingly open to supporting hybrid models, especially those that combine market mechanisms with measurable impact. For early-stage founders, grants can provide risk-tolerant capital that enables experimentation, product-market fit testing, and team building without the pressures of repayment or equity dilution. Program-related investments (PRIs), often made by foundations, blur the line further—offering low-interest loans or equity with impact-first expectations.

One notable example is the Skoll Foundation, which has supported hundreds of social entrepreneurs with unrestricted capital, often before mainstream investors recognised their potential. Skoll's approach is instructive: they fund leaders, not just metrics; vision, not just models. For founders seeking such support, the key lies in storytelling—conveying not only what the enterprise *does*, but why it exists, how it challenges systemic inequities, and what deeper shift it aims to catalyse. Grantmakers are not looking for transactional returns; they are investing in transformation.

Still, grants come with trade-offs. Application cycles can be lengthy, reporting requirements onerous, and renewal uncertain. Relying exclusively on them can limit autonomy and long-term sustainability. This is where equity and debt capital enter the picture—but with a twist.

For many mission-driven founders, the term "investor" evokes discomfort. Stories abound of venture capitalists who prioritise short-term scale over stakeholder well-being, or who impose governance structures that erode community voice. Yet not all investment is extractive. The rise of impact investing has introduced a new class of funders who seek blended returns—financial, social, and environmental. These investors are often willing to accept lower financial yields in exchange for meaningful, measurable impact. But finding the right partners requires discernment.

A successful example of ethical investment in practice is seen in the trajectory of Warby Parker, the eyewear company that embedded a one-for-one giving model into its operations. While now a public company, its early growth was fuelled by investors aligned with its social mission. Rather than chasing the fastest path to IPO, Warby Parker took time to refine its supply chain ethics, environmental footprint, and giving strategy. Its investors didn't merely tolerate this—they supported it, recognising that long-term value is built on trust, not speed.

Attracting such investors begins with clarity. Founders must articulate not only the financial mechanics of their business, but the non-negotiable ethical boundaries. What trade-offs are unacceptable? What timelines support both growth and integrity? What role will the investor play beyond capital? This level of transparency does more than protect the mission—it attracts the *right kind* of capital. Investors who understand that values are not a marketing strategy but the operating system of the enterprise.

One increasingly popular instrument in this space is revenue-based financing (RBF). Unlike traditional equity, RBF allows entrepreneurs to repay capital as a percentage of revenue—flexible, aligned with cash flow, and free from ownership dilution. This model is particularly suitable for mission-driven founders wary of giving up control. It also aligns incentives: investors succeed when the business thrives, but without demanding unsustainable growth.

Another innovative approach is community investment. Through direct public offerings, crowdfunding, or co-operative structures, enterprises raise capital from those they serve—building loyalty, embedding accountability, and distributing financial benefit. Examples include community solar initiatives, local food co-ops, and even equity crowdfunding platforms like Crowdcube and Seedrs. These models not only raise money—they deepen stakeholder engagement and ensure that economic value flows back into the communities creating it.

Creative financing also includes partnership models—where aligned organisations contribute resources, expertise, or infrastructure in lieu of capital. A purpose-led health tech startup might partner with a nonprofit hospital network for distribution, or an education platform might secure in-kind content from universities. These arrangements, while less visible than formal investments, can provide crucial early-stage momentum while reinforcing strategic alignment.

Still, amid all these options, caution is warranted. Not every grant is helpful. Not every investor is values-aligned. Not every dollar is worth accepting. Founders must be vigilant about *capital fit*—not just financial terms, but cultural congruence. Does the funder understand the community you serve? Do they share your sense of urgency? Will they stand by you during ambiguity, or push for pivots that betray your purpose?

The psychological dynamics of fundraising also deserve attention. Many social entrepreneurs struggle with the act of asking—perceiving it as begging, as compromise, or as distraction from the "real work." This mindset must be challenged. Fundraising is not extraction; it is invitation. It is the opportunity to enrol others in your vision, to build a shared stake in transformation. When done with clarity and authenticity, it becomes an extension of the mission itself.

In this regard, narrative matters. Investors and grantmakers alike respond to coherence: a financial model that supports the stated impact, a team that reflects the community it serves, a growth plan that is bold but believable. Numbers matter—but so does ethos. Founders who can articulate *how* their model works, *why* it matters, and *what* kind of support is required are far more likely to build sustainable funding partnerships.

Equally important is internal financial literacy. Founders must understand their own numbers—not just at a high level, but in detail. Unit economics, cash flow forecasts, cost structures, and break-even points are not investor jargon—they are tools of empowerment. They allow you to negotiate from a place of knowledge, to make offers and counter-offers that are strategic, and to remain in control of your company's future.

Ultimately, funding a mission-led enterprise is not about finding money—it is about *crafting alignment.* It is about designing a capital strategy that serves your purpose, sustains your people, and reflects your principles. It requires humility to learn, courage to say no, and vision to imagine alternatives.

In a financial world often defined by extraction, every ethical funding decision is a radical act. It says: we will not trade short-term gain for long-term harm. We will not sacrifice integrity at the altar of scale. We will build enterprises that are as thoughtful about how they are funded as they are about what they deliver.

That is the future of finance in a mission-driven economy. Not just smart capital—but conscious capital. Not just money that funds change—but money that *embodies* it.

Profit for Purpose: The Rise of Social Entrepreneurship

For much of modern economic history, business and philanthropy have been treated as distinct, even opposing, realms—one driven by profit, the other by purpose. The former was expected to generate wealth, the latter to redistribute it. Yet, in recent decades, a profound shift has begun to dismantle this binary. At the centre of this transformation is the rise of social entrepreneurship—a movement that reimagines the relationship between commerce and conscience, embedding social and environmental missions directly into the core of business models. Profit is no longer viewed as morally suspect, nor is impact seen as the domain of charity alone. Instead, we are witnessing the maturation of a new hybrid logic: *profit for purpose.*

Social entrepreneurship is not a trend—it is an evolutionary step in the history of capitalism. It reflects a growing societal consensus that the most pressing challenges of our time—inequality, climate change, education, healthcare access—cannot be solved by government and nonprofits alone. It also responds to a new generation of consumers, investors, and workers who demand more from the organisations they support. They want products that align with their values, jobs that offer meaning beyond salary, and investment portfolios that generate returns without complicity in harm. In this context, enterprises that integrate impact into their revenue models are not fringe experiments; they are the vanguard of a redefined economy.

At its core, social entrepreneurship is about alignment—between what a business does, how it earns money, and the change it seeks to create. It resists the old model where companies maximise profit in one domain and outsource conscience to corporate social responsibility departments or occasional donations. Instead, social enterprises treat impact as integral, not incidental. Their business activities *are* their interventions.

One of the most cited examples of this model is TOMS, the footwear company that popularised the "buy one, give one" approach. For every pair of shoes sold, another was donated to someone in need. While the model has evolved over time in response to criticism and learning, it sparked a global conversation about how consumerism could be leveraged for good. More importantly, it inspired hundreds of copycat and counter-models, each refining the concept of embedded impact.

Yet social entrepreneurship is not limited to cause marketing or donation-based models. Some of the most effective examples come from ventures that address systemic barriers through the very nature of their operations. Take d.light, a company providing affordable solar lighting solutions across Africa and South Asia. Its revenue comes from selling clean energy products, but its impact lies in displacing kerosene use, improving health outcomes, extending study hours for students, and empowering rural economies. The business is not merely funding impact—it *is* the impact.

Similarly, consider Toast Ale, a UK-based brewery that uses surplus bread to make beer, reducing food waste in the process. Its revenue model is indistinguishable from its environmental mission. The more beer it sells, the more bread is diverted from landfill. The integration is seamless, and the messaging is compelling: drinking beer can fight climate change. It's a model where commerce becomes activism, and consumers become co-conspirators in systems change.

This kind of alignment, however, is not accidental. It requires intentional design—what social impact theorist Jed Emerson has called "blended value" creation. Social entrepreneurs must ask not just how to make a product desirable, but how to ensure its creation, distribution, and consumption advance the intended impact. This involves deep attention to supply chains, pricing strategies, customer engagement, and governance structures. It is not enough to sell good things—you must *sell them well*, and ethically.

The process often requires navigating complex tensions. Should a social enterprise prioritise underserved markets, even if margins are lower? Should it accept investment from backers who may not share its values? Should it grow rapidly to increase reach, or slowly to preserve integrity? These questions do not have universal answers, but they demand a framework—one rooted in clarity of mission, transparency of trade-offs, and accountability to the communities being served.

Financially, profit-for-purpose ventures challenge conventional wisdom. They are often scrutinised more harshly than traditional businesses because they claim a moral high ground. This creates a double bind: succeed too visibly, and risk accusations of "selling out"; fail, and reinforce scepticism that mission cannot coexist with market logic. The antidote is nuance. Social entrepreneurs must reject purity tests while maintaining fidelity to their principles. Profit is not the problem; *unprincipled profit* is. When returns are generated through products and practices that uplift rather than exploit, there is no contradiction—only convergence.

The rise of legal structures such as benefit corporations (B Corps) reflects this changing ethos. B Corps are required to consider the impact of their decisions on workers, customers, suppliers, community, and the environment. This shifts fiduciary duty from shareholder primacy to stakeholder balance. Companies like Patagonia, Allbirds, and Ben & Jerry's have embraced this model, proving that ethics and enterprise can scale together. These are not philanthropic gestures—they are strategic choices that build trust, differentiate brands, and attract talent.

The investor landscape has also begun to respond. The global impact investing market has surpassed $1 trillion, with funds targeting both financial return and social outcome. This has enabled social enterprises to access capital on terms that reflect their hybrid identity. However, not all impact investors are created equal. Some still apply conventional return expectations while using the language of purpose. Founders must be vigilant in vetting capital partners, ensuring that their values are not compromised in pursuit of scale.

Equally significant is the rise of consumer-powered funding models. Crowdfunding platforms like Kickstarter, Indiegogo, and Seedrs have enabled thousands of social ventures to raise capital directly from their communities. These models not only finance businesses—they democratise ownership and deepen accountability. They signal that impact is not just a product to be consumed, but a project to be co-created.

For aspiring social entrepreneurs, the question is not merely how to monetise impact, but how to *operationalise* it. What does your business model do beyond sell? Whom does it empower? What systemic problem does it chip away at each time a transaction occurs? These are design questions, strategic questions, and moral questions. They demand a new literacy—a comfort with complexity, a tolerance for ambiguity, and a commitment to learning in public.

Social entrepreneurship is not a silver bullet. It will not singlehandedly dismantle structural oppression or reverse ecological collapse. But it is a critical lever—a way to redirect the immense power of markets toward the common good. It reclaims business as a vehicle for stewardship, not just accumulation. And it offers a blueprint for a future in which prosperity is not measured solely in pounds or profits, but in the depth and durability of our collective wellbeing.

The next frontier lies in systems thinking—moving beyond individual enterprises to ecosystems of aligned actors: funders, policymakers, educators, and consumers, all playing their part. The social entrepreneur of the future will not merely build a business; they will build *infrastructure* for equitable economies. They will move from isolated interventions to interdependent networks, from hero narratives to collective agency.

In this vision, profit is not the enemy of purpose. It is its enabler. When earned through intention, governed with accountability, and reinvested in justice, profit becomes a form of fuel—one that sustains not just ventures, but values.

This is the essence of profit for purpose. Not charity. Not compromise. But a conscious, courageous redesign of how business gets done—and why.

Money Myths That Keep Purpose-Driven People Broke

Within the impact economy, there exists a quiet epidemic—one that doesn't stem from a lack of passion or talent, but from a deeply embedded set of beliefs about money. Many purpose-driven entrepreneurs, despite their intelligence and dedication, find themselves chronically underpaid, under-resourced, or financially insecure. Not because their ideas lack merit, but because their relationship with money is riddled with misconceptions. These myths, often inherited from cultural narratives, social justice movements, or internalised moral codes, shape behaviours in ways that silently sabotage sustainability. Left unchallenged, they ensure that many of the world's most visionary changemakers remain on the financial margins of the very systems they are working to transform.

The myth most commonly encountered is the false dichotomy between doing good and doing well. Many founders, particularly in the nonprofit or social enterprise space, internalise the belief that financial success is somehow antithetical to moral integrity. They feel a tacit guilt about charging for their services, paying themselves market-rate salaries, or generating surplus revenue. Money becomes synonymous with compromise, or worse, corruption. Yet this thinking is not only outdated—it is deeply harmful.

Profit, in and of itself, is morally neutral. What gives it meaning is the process by which it is earned and the purpose to which it is applied. When revenue is generated through ethical practices, reinvested in mission, and used to support fair wages and community benefit, it becomes a force for dignity and self-determination. Underpricing, by contrast, often leads to overwork, burnout, and limited reach. It also sets a precedent that devalues impact work—sending the message that social outcomes are worth less than commercial ones. This undermines the very legitimacy of the purpose-driven economy.

A real-world example is illustrative. Consider a mental health startup offering subsidised counselling for marginalised communities. Initially, its founder charged minimal fees out of a sincere desire to remain accessible. But as demand grew and the team expanded, financial strain set in. The founder was working seventy-hour weeks, relying on volunteers, and unable to pay herself consistently. It wasn't until she restructured her pricing, introduced tiered access, and secured ethical grant funding that the model became viable. The service reached more people, her team stabilised, and the mission flourished—not despite charging more, but because she finally acknowledged that sustainability requires financial maturity.

Another pervasive myth is that money will dilute your mission. This is often rooted in fears of selling out, especially when external capital is involved. Founders worry that accepting investment will subject them to pressure for rapid growth, compromise their values, or shift focus away from the communities they serve. While these are legitimate concerns, they are not inevitable outcomes. The issue is not capital itself, but alignment. Purpose-led entrepreneurs must develop the discernment to distinguish between funding that supports their integrity and funding that erodes it.

Social enterprise founder Amanda Johnson offers a case in point. Her organic skincare company, rooted in environmental sustainability and equitable labour practices, declined multiple offers from investors who proposed rapid expansion via overseas outsourcing. Instead, she opted for a slower growth trajectory backed by impact-first capital from an ethical investment firm. The result was a company that scaled on its own terms—maintaining product quality, protecting supplier relationships, and building a fiercely loyal customer base. Her experience reinforces the truth that mission and money are only at odds when values are compromised at the negotiation table. Financial empowerment does not require surrendering your ethos; it requires asserting it clearly and early.

Then there is the martyrdom myth: the belief that struggle is a badge of honour. Many purpose-driven leaders operate with an unconscious conviction that suffering is part of the job—that sacrifice, not strategy, is the path to legitimacy. They equate personal depletion with dedication, treating exhaustion as evidence of commitment. This is not only psychologically damaging, but also strategically unsound. An exhausted leader cannot lead. A starved organisation cannot scale. A mission built on scarcity will replicate scarcity.

The nonprofit sector, in particular, has long been plagued by a culture of austerity. Low overhead is fetishised. Staff are expected to go above and beyond for substandard pay. Innovation is stifled by risk aversion. The result is not increased efficiency, but chronic instability. Respected organisations close their doors not because they lack vision, but because they never developed the financial infrastructure to withstand volatility. Martyrdom is not a business model. Resilience is.

To move beyond this pattern, founders must interrogate their beliefs about worth. If you believe that money is something you don't deserve, you will unconsciously sabotage opportunities to earn it. If you see financial planning as greedy or secondary, you will underinvest in the very systems that make your impact scalable. Cultivating financial literacy is not about becoming a finance expert—it is about reclaiming agency. It is about understanding the mechanics of sustainability so that your values can live not just in your messaging, but in your margins.

Another damaging assumption is that impact work should be free—or nearly so. This often arises in the social innovation sector, where consumers and funders alike have become conditioned to expect social goods at minimal cost. A purpose-driven tech platform is expected to offer free access to underserved users without compromising functionality. A coaching programme for at-risk youth is expected to deliver measurable outcomes on a shoestring budget. This double standard—where commercial ventures are rewarded for monetisation but impact ventures are punished for it—must be challenged.

The solution is to re-educate both internal and external stakeholders. Founders must learn to articulate the *real cost* of impact—not just in terms of outputs, but in terms of infrastructure, emotional labour, and time. They must also normalise the language of investment over donation, return over rescue. When pricing reflects value, the sector is elevated. When it does not, the work remains precarious.

This reframing must also extend to how purpose-led people think about wealth itself. Many carry the myth that wealth is inherently unjust—that to accumulate it is to betray the cause. But this ignores the reality that wealth is a tool. In the hands of values-driven leaders, it becomes a vehicle for systemic reinvestment. It allows for the redistribution of resources, the funding of overlooked projects, and the modelling of new economic norms. Refusing wealth out of fear or guilt doesn't dismantle injustice—it often perpetuates it by leaving capital in the hands of those less likely to use it wisely.

Impact investor Rodney Foxworth, founder of Worthmore Capital, has spoken candidly about this dilemma. He argues that for historically excluded communities, access to capital is not just a matter of equity—it is a matter of power. Building wealth within purpose-driven ecosystems is not selfish. It is strategic. It creates a counterweight to dominant capital structures and enables self-determination. Financial fluency is not betrayal. It is resistance.

The task, then, is to replace these myths with new mental models—models grounded in sustainability, alignment, and agency. Purpose-driven people must believe they can thrive, not just survive. They must see money as a means of amplifying their mission, not diluting it. They must understand that financial resilience is not a deviation from impact—it is what makes impact endure.

To do this requires a community-wide shift. Incubators, accelerators, and funders must dismantle the scarcity mindset baked into so many support systems. Financial education must become a core part of leadership development. And founders must give themselves permission to flourish—recognising that their wellbeing is not an indulgence, but a strategy.

Myths persist because they are repeated. They dissolve when challenged. And it is time—long past time—for purpose-led leaders to tell a different story about money. A story where financial strength is not a moral failing but a mission multiplier.

Where wealth, earned ethically, becomes a tool of empowerment. Where the changemakers shaping the world are no longer broke, burnt out, or barely hanging on—but fully resourced, deeply rooted, and ready to lead.

Interactive Exercise: Your Personal Financial Roadmap for Impact

For mission-driven entrepreneurs, aligning financial decisions with a sense of purpose is more than a noble ambition—it is an operational necessity. Yet, too often, the emotional pull of the mission eclipses the financial architecture needed to sustain it. Many founders find themselves in a reactive cycle: chasing grants, underpricing services, postponing salary, or delaying investments. These patterns are rarely the result of poor intention or laziness; rather, they stem from a lack of structure—a missing bridge between purpose and financial planning. This is where the concept of a *personal financial roadmap for impact* becomes not just useful, but transformative.

A financial roadmap, in this context, is not a traditional budget. It is a strategic framework designed to help founders clarify, organise, and operationalise their financial lives in service of their mission. It integrates personal needs, business realities, and impact goals into a cohesive whole. It is as much about psychology as it is about spreadsheets—because money, for the purpose-led, is never just about numbers. It is about meaning, boundaries, agency, and sustainability.

The first step in crafting a personal financial roadmap is to establish *clarity*. This may sound obvious, but many entrepreneurs operate with vague or inherited definitions of financial success. They set goals based on industry benchmarks or external pressures rather than internal needs. Clarity begins by asking foundational questions: What is your enough? What are your non-negotiables? How much do you need—monthly, annually—to live in alignment with your values, care for your health, support your family, and avoid burnout?

For instance, if your mission is to expand access to mental health services in underserved communities, but your personal income falls below the cost of living, your work is likely to be unsustainable in the long term. Worse, it may quietly erode your wellbeing and decision-making capacity. A founder who under-earns becomes vulnerable—not just financially, but emotionally and relationally. Clarity means understanding that self-neglect is not a strategy for impact. It is a form of slow sabotage.

The second component is *alignment*. This is where your personal financial needs and business model meet. Too often, founders separate the two—treating the business as a vehicle for service and their own needs as an afterthought. But the most resilient ventures are those where the founder's financial wellbeing is embedded, not bolted on. Alignment means designing a revenue model that allows you to earn what you need, without guilt or compromise.

Real-world examples bring this to life. Take the case of a founder running a purpose-led design agency working exclusively with nonprofits. Initially, her pricing reflected what she thought her clients could afford. She set low rates, absorbed extra labour, and deferred her salary. But as demand grew and stress mounted, she realised the model was unsustainable. With the help of a coach, she recalculated her pricing based on her actual needs, team costs, and growth targets. She introduced a tiered fee structure, offered discounted rates to smaller clients through partnerships, and began paying herself a consistent income. The result wasn't just stability—it was relief. And her clients respected the transparency and professionalism of her new approach.

This highlights the critical insight: financial integrity is part of your brand. It signals to clients, investors, and collaborators that you respect your work, your team, and your future. Alignment is not about maximising revenue at all costs. It is about ensuring that your financial systems are structured to uphold—not undermine—your mission.

Once alignment is in place, the next element is *forecasting*. This moves you from short-term survival to long-term vision. Financial forecasting is not about prediction; it's about *preparation*. It allows you to map income streams, anticipate expenses, and identify key decision points in advance. For purpose-driven leaders, this means asking: What will my cash flow look like during low revenue months? What funding milestones must I hit to expand my impact? What reserves do I need to withstand an economic shock?

These are not pessimistic questions—they are responsible ones. A well-constructed financial forecast can reveal when to raise prices, when to hire, when to seek investment, or when to pause. It prevents overextension and fosters confident, values-aligned decision-making. It also makes your mission more investable. Funders are far more likely to support a visionary leader with a coherent financial strategy than one operating on instinct alone.

However, no roadmap is complete without addressing *psychological blocks*. Many purpose-led entrepreneurs carry limiting beliefs about money—often unconsciously. These may include guilt about charging, fear of visibility, resistance to wealth, or anxiety about asking for help. Without addressing these beliefs, even the best strategy will falter. A founder may underquote out of fear of rejection, overdeliver to justify their price, or delay growth because they don't feel ready. These behaviours are not financial—they are emotional. And they require deliberate reflection.

One practical exercise is to journal your personal money story: What messages did you internalise about money growing up? How did your culture, religion, or education shape your beliefs about wealth? What patterns do you notice in how you earn, spend, or give? By naming these narratives, you can begin to choose which ones to keep—and which to rewrite. Financial empowerment is as much about emotional fluency as it is about arithmetic.

This brings us to the final, and perhaps most empowering, part of the roadmap: *agency*. Your roadmap is not a static plan—it is a living document. It should evolve with your goals, context, and capacity. It should be revisited quarterly, adjusted annually, and used as a tool for reflection and course correction. It should also include built-in checkpoints: Are your financial goals still aligned with your mission? Are you honouring your own limits? Are you investing in yourself—skills, rest, support—as much as in your business?

One founder I worked with created a ritual around her financial review. Each quarter, she booked a weekend away—no meetings, no social media, just her, her numbers, and her vision. She reviewed income, expenses, progress on savings, and upcoming goals. But she also reflected on her emotional relationship with money: Was she feeling abundant or anxious? Empowered or depleted? These reviews became sacred time—not just for bookkeeping, but for recalibration.

Incorporating these reflections into your own roadmap shifts your financial planning from a reactive chore to a strategic ritual. It becomes an act of leadership—an embodiment of the very principles you espouse. Because if your mission is about dignity, equity, or wellbeing, your financial practices must reflect those same values.

At a systems level, widespread adoption of personal financial roadmaps within the impact sector could shift the entire culture. It would normalise sustainability over sacrifice. It would empower founders to say no to misaligned funding. It would increase the longevity of purpose-driven ventures and improve the wellbeing of those who lead them. It would challenge the myth that impact work must always operate from lack.

This is the deeper promise of the financial roadmap: not just clarity, not just control, but coherence. A life where your money supports your mission, and your mission is not threatened by your money. A life where purpose and prosperity are not adversaries, but allies. A life designed—not by default, but by intention.

Such a life is not only possible—it is necessary. Because the world needs mission-driven people who are not just inspired, but resourced. Not just driven, but grounded. And not just surviving—but building with confidence, clarity, and compassion. Your roadmap is the tool. The destination is yours to define.

Chapter 7
The Mission-Mapping Framework

Mission, by its nature, carries a certain electricity. It motivates, galvanises, sometimes even blinds. But raw drive alone won't carry an entrepreneur the distance. Without a deliberate architecture to hold it, even the most heartfelt purpose can start to drift—quietly, imperceptibly—until one day it no longer resembles the vision that sparked it. The real challenge isn't finding the fire. It's giving it form. It's weaving aspiration into execution, and meaning into mechanisms that can withstand the wear of time. Chapter 7 introduces such a structure. The Mission-Mapping Framework is less a plan and more a compass—designed to guide entrepreneurs in aligning their deeper values with everyday decisions, financial models, and the evolving realities of leading with purpose.

Unlike conventional strategy templates—the sort that kick off with SWOT charts or business canvases—mission-mapping begins elsewhere. At a more human, less sanitised place. It starts with you. Not the version on a pitch deck, but the version who wakes up at 3am wondering if all this effort is actually adding up to something worthwhile. The framework opens with questions few founders are formally asked: What does fulfilment really mean for you? What legacy are you quietly hoping to leave behind? And perhaps most provocatively—what lines are you unwilling to cross, even in pursuit of scale or legitimacy? These aren't idle reflections; they're structural. Because when your business is designed in a vacuum, detached from the life it's meant to support, tension is guaranteed. But when the two are integrated with care, something remarkable happens: coherence.

At the centre of the framework are five guiding pillars—not rigid doctrines, but principles alive to context: Clarity, Coherence, Capacity, Continuity, and Contribution. Each touches a vital thread in the tapestry of mission-led leadership. Clarity, first and foremost, is about rootedness—knowing who you are, what you stand for, and what specific imprint you intend to leave. Coherence ensures that your values aren't just broadcast in lofty statements, but embedded—often invisibly—in how you price your services, choose your collaborators, and structure your team. Capacity is the often-overlooked engine room: your emotional resilience, financial buffers, and relational depth that allow you to show up without burning out. Continuity reminds us that adaptability isn't drift—it's design, a way of bending without breaking as external circumstances evolve. And Contribution—perhaps the heartbeat of the whole structure—reorients your work toward service, anchoring it in value that matters to both you and those you serve.

These pillars do more than decorate theory. They underpin what may be one of the most underused strategies in impact-driven work: reverse engineering fulfilment. Too many ventures are launched in response to trends, funding cycles, or perceived opportunity gaps. Rarely do founders begin by asking themselves what kind of life they're trying to build—what, ten years from now, would make this journey feel deeply worth it. And yet, that's precisely what the most grounded leaders do. They start not with a business plan, but with a vision of a life well lived. Then they build backwards.

Picture this: a founder dreams of spending several months each year volunteering abroad with their children. That vision alone reshapes the entire business model—timelines, staffing, cash flow, everything. Now imagine another founder with ambitions of global scale and a sprawling team. Both are valid. Neither is "more impact-driven." But the difference lies in intentionality. Reverse engineering asks not, "What's the next move?" but "What kind of life would this work need to make possible to be truly meaningful?"

That shift in orientation reframes how decisions are made. Once you're clear on what you're really building toward—not just in terms of KPIs or market share, but felt experience—priorities come into focus. You start saying no, not out of fear, but from conviction. You stop benchmarking against someone else's trajectory. The noise dies down. Your own voice grows louder.

But vision, if it stays trapped in the abstract, can become a kind of quiet torment. That's where articulation comes in—specifically through what this chapter calls a money mission statement. Unlike traditional financial plans, which fixate on goals, projections, and bottom lines, this statement pulls your financial decisions into direct conversation with your purpose. It makes explicit why you earn, spend, save, and invest—not in theoretical terms, but in ways that illuminate what really matters to you.

One might sound like: "I earn through ethical entrepreneurship to create a life of spaciousness, fund regenerative projects, and model fair economics in my sector." Another might declare: "I seek financial independence not as an escape, but as a platform for influence—to uplift marginalised voices and challenge scarcity mindsets." These aren't affirmations. They're anchors. They tether the financial machinery of your business to its moral architecture. They lend integrity to hard decisions, be it turning down a misaligned investor or rethinking your compensation strategy.

And then—because thinking alone changes little—the chapter offers a tool to bring it all into the real. The Mission-Mapping Blueprint is not some fill-in-the-blanks worksheet. It's a strategy tool designed for nuance. It walks you through defining your core values, crafting your life vision, clarifying your impact priorities, reckoning with your current financial state, and surfacing leverage points for more aligned action. The aim isn't precision. It's pattern recognition. It's seeing where your systems reinforce your purpose—and where they quietly undermine it.

Consider the founder who, after completing this process, realised her consultancy was optimised entirely around external perception. Her days revolved around lead generation and digital presence, but her heart was elsewhere: in creating generational change for her community. That insight led to radical shifts. She began hiring and mentoring local talent, implemented a profit-sharing model, and dropped a few big-ticket clients who conflicted with her values. The result? A business that felt like her. Profitable, yes—but also grounded, generous, and deeply personal.

Another founder, in mapping his fulfilment vision, recognised that his dream included space—room to write, to spend time with his children, to think without interruption. None of those things were remotely present in his current operations. So he restructured: introduced automation, trained an associate to handle onboarding, reoriented his schedule. The business grew, modestly. But he stopped fantasising about escape. His company became a wellspring rather than a weight.

These are not outliers. They're signals. Evidence that when purpose is deliberately translated into practice, things begin to shift. There's less scatter. Fewer decisions made from panic or comparison. And more from a place of grounded strategy. Founders move from firefighting to focused execution. From scrambling toward relevance to building from conviction. The enterprises they lead don't just reflect their values—they reinforce them.

And that, ultimately, is what the Mission-Mapping Framework is about. It's not another exercise in branding or productivity. It's a reclamation—of direction, of meaning, of the right to design a life and business that feel not just impressive, but coherent. It challenges the tyranny of borrowed metrics. It invites a more honest accounting of what success looks and feels like—on your own terms.

In a culture that rewards speed, visibility, and ever-more growth, this approach is quietly radical. To embed fulfilment at the very heart of your financial model is to reject the idea that purpose must be squeezed in at the margins. It is to insist that meaning and money can—and must—coexist, not in conflict, but in choreography.

This chapter offers a map. But more importantly, it invites a new kind of travel. Not toward a version of success borrowed from the world around you, but toward one designed—deliberately, courageously—on your own terms. With structure. With strategy. And with a mission that doesn't just live in vision statements, but breathes through every corner of your work.

The Five Pillars of Mission-Driven Success

Sustaining a mission-driven enterprise over time requires more than conviction, creativity, or even capital. It requires *cohesion*—a deliberate architecture that links purpose, operations, and financial sustainability in a dynamic and enduring structure. Too often, founders begin with inspiration and rely on improvisation. But even the most powerful purpose will eventually fragment if it is not supported by a resilient, repeatable, and reflective framework. The Five Pillars of Mission-Driven Success offer such a foundation—a comprehensive yet flexible system for ensuring that a mission-led business can grow without losing its soul, scale without compromising its integrity, and generate income without diluting its impact.

The first pillar is **Clarity**. Without a crystal-clear articulation of your mission, every decision becomes a negotiation, every opportunity a potential derailment. Clarity is not merely a slogan—it is a strategic filter. It defines what you stand for, whom you serve, and what you are building beyond profit. It is the difference between being pulled in multiple directions and staying centred in purpose. Clarity also extends beyond language to *action*. A founder may say they care about environmental justice, but if their supply chain decisions are based purely on cost, the signal is inconsistent. The enterprises that succeed over time are those whose internal logic—values, voice, and value proposition—are aligned with precision.

Consider the example of Too Good To Go, a mobile platform that connects users with surplus food from restaurants, cafes, and bakeries to prevent waste. Their mission—fighting food waste at scale—is not only clear but evident in every facet of their business model. From UX design to partner onboarding to marketing, their operations reflect their commitment to reducing environmental harm. This clarity has allowed them to expand across multiple countries while maintaining consistent messaging and engagement. When your mission is this clear, it becomes a magnet—for customers, employees, funders, and collaborators who share your vision.

The second pillar is **Coherence**. Whereas clarity defines what you do and why, coherence ensures that your strategies, systems, and behaviours consistently reflect that purpose. Incoherence is one of the most corrosive threats to a mission-driven organisation. It breeds internal confusion, damages trust, and fractures morale. Coherence requires a deep commitment to internal alignment—not only between departments or goals, but between *intentions and operations*. It demands that your pricing reflects your values, your hiring reflects your culture, and your communication reflects your truth.

Patagonia exemplifies coherence. Their commitment to environmental activism is not a side project—it is built into their product sourcing, supply chain transparency, and even their political lobbying. When the company decided to donate its entire $10 million tax cut to grassroots environmental organisations, it wasn't a PR stunt—it was a logical expression of their coherence. Such decisions strengthen trust, brand equity, and internal morale. Coherence, when fully embodied, becomes a powerful differentiator in a world saturated with performative ethics.

The third pillar is **Capacity**. Vision without capacity is a recipe for burnout and stagnation. Capacity refers to the internal resources—financial, emotional, human, and operational—that enable a mission to be sustained and expanded. Too often, founders assume that passion will carry them through resource constraints. While passion may ignite action, only capacity ensures its longevity. This means building systems that reduce founder dependency, developing financial buffers, and cultivating a team culture that supports health as much as performance.

A revealing case is that of the social enterprise Greyston Bakery in New York. Known for its "open hiring" model—where anyone can get a job without background checks, interviews, or resumes—Greyston's mission is to provide employment opportunities to those typically excluded from the labour market. Yet the brilliance of their model lies not just in its idealism, but in its operational rigour. They have invested deeply in workforce support programmes, mentorship, and internal training to ensure employees succeed. They understand that impact cannot flourish without infrastructure. Their mission is sustained not by charity, but by capacity—systems that make their ideals operationally viable.

The fourth pillar is **Continuity**. A mission-led business must be resilient in the face of change—economic shocks, political shifts, leadership transitions, or personal evolution. Continuity refers to the ability to adapt without losing the core DNA of the organisation. It requires structures that are flexible, values that are non-negotiable, and a long-term orientation that transcends short-term pressures. Continuity is not about resisting change; it is about preserving essence *through* change.

This is particularly evident in the evolution of the Aravind Eye Care System in India. Founded with the mission to eradicate needless blindness, Aravind has scaled into one of the world's largest and most efficient eye care systems. Yet despite its growth—from a single hospital to a network serving millions annually—it has never compromised its core commitment to accessibility and affordability. It maintains a cross-subsidisation model, where paying patients fund free care for those who cannot pay. Its operations have been refined, technologies updated, and systems modernised—but its mission remains intact. This is continuity in action: evolving wisely while holding fast to the ethical core.

The fifth and final pillar is **Contribution**. This pillar is both outcome and compass. It reminds entrepreneurs that mission is not self-referential—it exists to serve others, solve problems, and generate collective benefit. Contribution measures success not only in revenue or scale, but in lives touched, systems changed, and futures made possible. A focus on contribution prevents the enterprise from collapsing into ego, metrics obsession, or performative altruism. It also ensures that financial success is grounded in value creation, not extraction.

Tony's Chocolonely, a Dutch chocolate company, has built its entire brand around the commitment to a slave-free chocolate industry. They not only source ethically but advocate for systemic reform in cocoa supply chains. Their contribution goes beyond fair trade—it extends to changing consumer awareness, pressuring competitors, and shifting industry norms. Their growth is not accidental; it is fuelled by the authenticity of their contribution.

When these five pillars—clarity, coherence, capacity, continuity, and contribution—are actively developed, a mission-led business becomes more than a passion project. It becomes an institution. It earns the resilience to withstand pressure, the credibility to attract support, and the strategic maturity to grow without losing its soul. These pillars are not boxes to be ticked. They are disciplines to be cultivated. And they demand ongoing reflection, adjustment, and investment.

Founders and leaders who embed these principles into their decision-making processes gain more than efficiency—they gain *integrity*. Their enterprises become mirrors of their values and engines of systemic change. This is not merely about surviving in a competitive landscape. It is about *shaping* that landscape so that it becomes more just, more inclusive, and more aligned with the future we are trying to create.

Ultimately, the Five Pillars of Mission-Driven Success offer a roadmap—not toward ease, but toward coherence. A mission-led life or enterprise will always involve tension. But with these pillars in place, that tension becomes creative rather than destructive. It becomes a force that drives innovation, deepens reflection, and sustains commitment. And it allows purpose to move from inspiration to institution—from idea to infrastructure.

Reverse Engineering Fulfilment: Start With the End in Mind

In a world that champions momentum over mindfulness, many entrepreneurs find themselves in a constant state of forward motion—building, scaling, hiring, innovating—without ever pausing to ask where they are actually heading. It is an all-too-common paradox of modern business: individuals set out to create freedom, impact, and meaning, only to be consumed by the machinery of their own creation. Their calendars overflow, their personal lives contract, and their original vision fades into the background of quarterly goals and investor updates. The antidote is deceptively simple but deeply radical: start with the end in mind. Reverse engineering fulfilment is not a productivity hack. It is a design principle—an invitation to construct a business, financial system, and life that is architected around your ultimate definition of success.

This approach challenges the linear logic that dominates conventional entrepreneurship, where success is typically defined by growth metrics—revenue, reach, valuation—and only later, perhaps, adjusted to include purpose or lifestyle. Instead, it proposes a model in which fulfilment is the primary design constraint. Rather than asking, "What's next?" we ask, "What would make all of this worthwhile?" Rather than plotting a path to arbitrary benchmarks, we begin by vividly imagining the life we want to inhabit ten, twenty, or thirty years from now—and then design backwards.

At the heart of this practice is *clarity of vision*, not just for the business, but for the founder's whole life. Fulfilment is not compartmentalised. It includes how we spend our days, how we feel in our bodies, how connected we are to those we love, and whether our work is a source of nourishment or depletion. Too often, purpose-driven individuals are so focused on service to others that they neglect their own wellbeing. They confuse sacrifice with significance. But a depleted founder cannot sustain impact. Reverse engineering fulfilment requires us to define what a *sustainable, meaningful, joy-infused life* actually looks like—not in vague terms, but with granularity.

For instance, one might envision living in a specific location, working no more than thirty hours per week, earning enough to fund travel, family support, or philanthropy, and leading a team that shares decision-making power. Another might dream of building a school, retiring early to mentor young changemakers, or spending half the year in creative retreat. These visions are not indulgent—they are compass points. They allow us to evaluate present-day decisions not just in terms of efficiency, but in terms of resonance.

The power of this framework becomes clear when contrasted with founders who lack this long-range orientation. Take the case of a tech entrepreneur who scaled a social impact platform rapidly, won acclaim, attracted venture capital, and built a team of fifty—only to find herself mired in bureaucracy, distanced from the communities she once served, and unsure how to reclaim the autonomy she had initially sought. Her fulfilment had been deferred, outsourced to some mythical future when "things calmed down." But growth had become its own trap. Had she begun by defining her non-negotiables—creative autonomy, proximity to users, lean operations—her decisions would have taken a different shape.

By contrast, purpose-led entrepreneur Daniel Flynn, co-founder of Thankyou, a social enterprise in Australia, has consistently demonstrated this reverse-engineering mindset. Rather than pursuing scale at all costs, Thankyou made the counterintuitive decision to pause operations in some sectors until the model could align fully with its values. Flynn and his team walked away from short-term gains in favour of long-term coherence. Their ultimate goal was not just product sales, but authentic impact and systems change. That clarity allowed them to endure criticism, navigate uncertainty, and maintain mission fidelity under pressure.

Reverse engineering fulfilment also reshapes how we think about money. Financial goals are no longer standalone targets—they are tied to experiences, needs, and legacies. A business that generates £500,000 per year might be insufficient if it demands eighty-hour weeks and constant travel. Conversely, a business that generates £150,000 but allows for spaciousness, family time, and philanthropic giving might represent a far greater success—depending on the founder's criteria. When money is placed in the context of meaning, it becomes a servant, not a master. It becomes a resource for building a life on your own terms.

This perspective requires a shift in metrics. Rather than defaulting to revenue growth or customer acquisition as the only indicators of success, founders must consider metrics such as energy levels, joy, integrity, and community impact. These are harder to quantify but more reliable predictors of long-term viability. A company that generates revenue at the cost of its founder's health or its team's cohesion is not truly sustainable—no matter what the balance sheet says.

In practice, reverse engineering fulfilment involves structured reflection. Founders can begin by writing a detailed narrative of their ideal day, five or ten years from now. Where are you? What are you doing? Who are you with? What problems are you solving—and which have you stopped trying to fix? This exercise reveals embedded values, unmet desires, and unconscious assumptions. It can expose how much of your current trajectory is driven by default settings—social expectations, investor demands, legacy industry norms—rather than deliberate choice.

From there, a gap analysis can be conducted. What elements of that future vision already exist in your life? What feels radically distant? Where are the tensions? This is not a one-time exercise but a continuous discipline. As life evolves, so too does our definition of fulfilment. Children grow, priorities shift, global crises interrupt. The goal is not to lock yourself into a rigid blueprint, but to stay in dialogue with your evolving self—and to make strategic decisions accordingly.

The benefits of this approach extend beyond personal wellbeing. Teams led by founders who have reverse-engineered their fulfilment tend to be more focused, transparent, and resilient. When a leader knows what matters most to them, they are less likely to chase shiny distractions, overextend resources, or compromise on core values. They model intentionality, which cultivates trust. They also create space for others to define their own fulfilment, fostering a culture that honours whole humans—not just productivity units.

Moreover, funders and partners increasingly value this clarity. A founder who can articulate how their business model supports their life vision is not seen as selfish, but as strategic. It signals foresight, stability, and a commitment to sustainability. It invites collaboration based on alignment, not desperation. In the impact sector especially, where burnout is rampant and missions are emotionally taxing, this approach is not a luxury—it is a necessity.

There are, of course, challenges. Reverse engineering fulfilment may require difficult choices: declining high-profile opportunities, resisting pressure to scale, or walking away from revenue streams that conflict with your values. It may mean saying no to clients, partnerships, or media that dilute your voice. It requires courage—to disappoint others, to redefine success, to risk misunderstanding. But the reward is immense: a life and enterprise that feel like extensions of your deepest truth.

Ultimately, starting with the end in mind is not about arriving at a fixed destination. It is about building a compass—a way to navigate complexity with intention. It is about living in integrity with yourself while contributing meaningfully to the world. It is about designing a life where fulfilment is not a side effect of success, but its very definition.

In a landscape that rewards speed and visibility, choosing to reverse engineer your fulfilment is an act of defiance—and of wisdom. It signals that you are not merely reacting to opportunity, but shaping it. That your impact is not performative, but grounded. And that you are building not just a business, but a legacy—one that begins with vision, and is realised through every choice you make along the way.

Your Money Mission Statement: Defining Financial Goals That Feel Meaningful

Most people carry a financial narrative, yet few have taken the time to articulate a financial philosophy. They may have goals—earn more, save more, invest more—but they often lack a unifying principle that explains *why* those goals matter and how they connect to a broader life purpose. In the absence of this clarity, money becomes either a source of anxiety or an end in itself. It floats unmoored from meaning, driving decisions that feel logical but hollow. This is where the concept of a *Money Mission Statement* becomes indispensable. It offers not only clarity but coherence—linking financial decisions to deeply held values and providing a compass for building wealth with purpose.

Unlike a conventional financial plan, which emphasises numbers, timelines, and returns, a Money Mission Statement prioritises alignment. It asks not just "What do I want to achieve financially?" but "What kind of life am I trying to create, and how can my financial choices support that?" It's a declaration of intent—specific enough to guide decisions, flexible enough to evolve, and profound enough to reflect who you are beyond your balance sheet.

At its core, a Money Mission Statement integrates three dimensions: personal values, desired impact, and financial strategy. These elements do not exist in isolation. They inform and shape one another. For example, a commitment to environmental sustainability might shape not only your spending habits but also your investment portfolio and pricing model. A desire to spend more time with family might influence how you structure your business revenue streams. A passion for educational equity might direct surplus income toward scholarships, mentorship programmes, or community development. Money becomes not a goal, but a medium for expressing who you are and what matters most.

To understand the power of such a statement, consider the case of Jessica Norwood, founder of RUNWAY, a financial innovation firm that invests in Black entrepreneurs. Her Money Mission is rooted in reimagining capital access through a lens of cultural respect and restorative economics. Her financial decisions—from deploying patient capital to building community wealth—are not just tactical. They are deeply philosophical. They reflect a refusal to perpetuate extraction and a commitment to economic justice. Her wealth strategy is an ethical framework, not a neutral tool.

Contrast this with the experience of many early-stage entrepreneurs who pursue revenue without anchoring it in purpose. They chase growth, accumulate clients, or pivot endlessly in pursuit of traction—often ending up financially stretched and emotionally detached. When asked why they are pursuing their current model, they struggle to answer beyond "because it's what's working" or "because the market wants it." Without a Money Mission Statement, financial strategies are easily shaped by external pressure and short-term gain rather than intrinsic motivation or long-term vision.

Crafting a Money Mission Statement begins with deep self-inquiry. What are the values you hold sacred? What does a fulfilled life look like—not in abstract terms, but in tangible detail? What are the financial milestones that would enable that life, and why do they matter? These are not superficial questions. They demand honesty, courage, and a willingness to challenge inherited assumptions. Many of us have absorbed unexamined narratives about money—that it is scarce, that it must be hoarded, that it corrupts, or that it must always be given away. These beliefs shape behaviour in subtle but profound ways. Clarifying your Money Mission allows you to surface, scrutinise, and selectively discard these narratives in favour of ones that align with your evolving identity and purpose.

A powerful example comes from the social entrepreneur Sam Polk, who left a career on Wall Street to co-found Everytable, a food company that provides affordable, healthy meals in underserved communities. His Money Mission Statement might be summarised as: "I use financial tools to dismantle inequality and create access to dignity." This mission informs not only Everytable's pricing model—based on local community income—but also its franchise strategy, which empowers community members to become business owners. Polk's approach to wealth is not antithetical to profitability; it is grounded in a broader moral calculus. He is not *against* making money. He is committed to making it *mean* something.

For purpose-driven entrepreneurs, this distinction is crucial. Money is not inherently virtuous or corrupt. It is a force—a magnifier. When guided by a clear mission, it becomes a lever for agency, justice, creativity, and freedom. When unmoored from purpose, it becomes a source of drift, distraction, and often disillusionment. Your Money Mission Statement becomes the through-line that ensures consistency across domains: how you price your offerings, how you invest your profits, how you pay your team, and how you allocate your time.

It also serves as a vital communication tool. When clearly articulated, it can galvanise teams, attract aligned investors, and build trust with customers. In a world increasingly sceptical of performative ethics, authenticity matters. A founder who can say, "Here's how our financial model supports our mission" is more likely to be believed—and supported—than one who relies on vague notions of impact. The statement provides a narrative backbone, making it easier to explain trade-offs, justify pricing decisions, or resist pressure to conform to extractive norms.

There is also a practical benefit. A well-defined Money Mission Statement simplifies decision-making. When faced with an enticing contract, a lucrative but misaligned partnership, or an opportunity to scale quickly at the expense of your wellbeing, your mission becomes a touchstone. It helps you distinguish between "profitable" and "right for me." It encourages you to ask not only "Can I afford this?" but "Does this serve my purpose?" It reduces decision fatigue by filtering noise through meaning.

Yet, crafting such a statement is not a one-off task. It is a living declaration, one that should be revisited regularly as your circumstances evolve. A single parent running a mission-led consultancy will likely define financial meaning differently from a twenty-five-year-old launching a tech-for-good startup. And both may revise their statements as they move through different life stages, experience growth, encounter failure, or deepen their understanding of impact. The Money Mission Statement is not fixed; it is faithful. It evolves in tandem with your values and your vision.

To create one, begin by writing freely about your financial goals—without judgement. Then, interrogate those goals: What is underneath the desire for a six-figure income or a year of savings? What feeling, experience, or opportunity are you hoping to unlock? Next, identify the values that show up repeatedly in your writing—freedom, justice, generosity, creativity, security—and examine how they might be woven into your financial strategy. Finally, distil your insights into a statement that feels both aspirational and actionable. It might sound like:

"I build wealth to create time freedom, fund community-led initiatives, and model ethical entrepreneurship for future generations."

Or:

"My financial strategy is rooted in simplicity, sufficiency, and sovereignty—allowing me to live creatively, give abundantly, and invest in systems change."

The goal is not perfection. The goal is resonance. A Money Mission Statement should feel like an articulation of something you've always known but perhaps never named. It should make your decisions feel less like guesswork and more like expression. It should remind you that financial planning is not separate from your deeper work—it is part of it.

In an era where financial goals are often set for optics, status, or performance metrics, reclaiming the language of meaning is a radical act. It is an act of authorship. Of saying: I will not chase metrics that don't matter to me. I will not defer my joy, or my values, or my health for a version of success that leaves me hollow. I will define my own terms, and I will design a financial life that serves them.

Your Money Mission Statement is not a substitute for financial literacy or strategic planning. It is the soul of both. It ensures that every budget, investment, or pricing strategy is connected to something more enduring than profit: a life of purpose, coherence, and contribution. When money becomes a tool for meaning, we stop surviving and start *designing*—not just businesses, but futures worth believing in.

Interactive Exercise: Mission-Mapping Blueprint

Bridging purpose and profitability is no longer the exclusive domain of social enterprises or philanthropic ventures—it is fast becoming the strategic imperative for any individual or organisation seeking longevity, relevance, and integrity in their work. Yet for many purpose-led entrepreneurs, this integration remains an abstract ideal. They possess a strong internal compass, they know what they stand for, and they may even have a clear financial plan. But the connective tissue between vision and execution is often missing. The Mission-Mapping Blueprint is designed to address that gap: a strategic tool for translating ideals into infrastructure, and purpose into practical, financially viable models.

At its essence, mission-mapping is about systematising coherence. It acknowledges that good intentions alone do not lead to meaningful outcomes—especially in the complex terrain of entrepreneurship. A founder may be committed to sustainability, equity, or empowerment, but without aligning their pricing model, growth strategy, resource allocation, and operational rhythms with those commitments, the result is often misalignment, burnout, or mission drift. The blueprint provides a scaffold for intentionality. It helps individuals identify where purpose and profit are already working in harmony—and where subtle or significant misalignments threaten to undermine long-term success.

The process begins with an anchor: *the personal mission statement.* This is not a company tagline or elevator pitch, but a distilled articulation of what the entrepreneur wants their life's work to represent. This statement should address the type of impact they want to have, the legacy they want to leave, and the non-negotiables that must guide every business decision. For instance, an entrepreneur might declare: "My work exists to build community resilience, create intergenerational wealth in underserved populations, and model business as a tool for liberation." With this anchor in place, each subsequent decision—around funding, hiring, scaling, and even exiting—can be assessed for alignment.

The next layer is *clarifying financial needs and aspirations.* Too often, entrepreneurs design business models without any reference to their personal financial requirements, resulting in either overextension or unnecessary austerity. Mission mapping asks the entrepreneur to define what financial sustainability looks like in concrete terms. How much income do they need to live well and work ethically? What buffers and reserves are necessary to reduce stress and support creativity? What investments will enable the enterprise to thrive across business cycles? These questions move the financial conversation away from generic success metrics toward personal sufficiency and strategic foresight.

Real-world case studies reveal how transformative this clarity can be. Consider a health coach who launched her business with the mission of empowering marginalised women to reclaim their wellbeing. Initially, her services were priced well below market, driven by a desire for accessibility. However, within eighteen months, she was overworked, underpaid, and facing serious burnout. Through a mission-mapping exercise, she realised that sustaining her impact required a pricing model that honoured both accessibility and abundance. She introduced a sliding scale, added a group programme to reduce 1:1 time, and secured grant funding to sponsor underserved clients. Her mission didn't change—but her financial architecture matured to support it.

From this point, the blueprint moves into *mapping impact pathways*. This involves identifying the specific levers through which the business delivers value—not just to customers, but to the ecosystem. These pathways may include education, employment, community reinvestment, environmental stewardship, or cultural restoration. By explicitly naming these mechanisms, entrepreneurs can more easily assess whether their business model is supporting or diluting their impact. This also provides a foundation for communicating value to funders, partners, and customers in terms that transcend financial return.

An excellent example of this approach can be seen in the business model of Alaffia, a social enterprise that produces fair trade beauty and wellness products. Its impact pathways include employment for women in Togo, maternal health funding, and education infrastructure. These are not peripheral initiatives—they are embedded into how the company operates and earns. Their mission map is visible in every transaction, enabling customers to participate in the impact rather than simply observe it.

Another component of the Mission-Mapping Blueprint is *value-based decision-making frameworks.* Entrepreneurs must routinely navigate complexity—balancing urgency and importance, intuition and data, short-term gains and long-term vision. Without a system to filter these choices, decision fatigue and reactive thinking can easily lead to compromises that chip away at mission integrity. A values-aligned decision matrix, integrated into the blueprint, offers clarity. For instance, when faced with a potential funding offer, the founder can ask: Does this partner share our core commitments? Will this funding pressure us to prioritise growth over depth? Will it allow us to maintain transparency and accountability?

This becomes particularly important in moments of opportunity or crisis. One entrepreneur who followed a mission-mapping process was later approached by a multinational firm offering a lucrative acquisition. On the surface, the offer promised stability and scale. But using her blueprint, she realised that the acquiring company's values and track record clashed with her vision for ethical labour and community ownership. She declined the deal. While difficult, the decision preserved her company's identity, and within a year, she secured alternative funding from a mission-aligned impact investor who respected her commitment to autonomy and local economic empowerment.

The final segment of the blueprint involves *integrating operational structures with mission outcomes*. This is where abstract values become concrete strategies. It includes evaluating hiring practices to ensure representation and equity, designing KPIs that measure mission impact alongside revenue, and ensuring team incentives are aligned with purpose. It also means building systems of reflection—regular check-ins, financial reviews, and impact audits—to ensure that the map is not static but adaptive.

One of the most effective implementations of this idea is seen in the approach of the cooperative business sector. Worker-owned co-ops such as Up & Go, a platform of cleaning service providers in New York City, integrate mission and operations seamlessly. Decisions are made collectively, profits are distributed equitably, and the customer experience is shaped by a commitment to dignity, not just efficiency. Their blueprint is baked into their bylaws, onboarding, and communications—not as a branding exercise, but as an operational ethos.

To support readers in applying the blueprint themselves, the chapter culminates in a guided exercise. This interactive component invites readers to articulate their mission, define their financial thresholds for sustainability, trace their impact pathways, establish decision filters, and conduct an operational audit. Rather than overwhelming them with checklists, the exercise encourages deep reflection, offering prompts that require readers to slow down, tune in, and name what truly matters. The intention is not perfection—it is alignment.

Ultimately, the Mission-Mapping Blueprint is more than a strategic tool. It is a declaration of coherence. It affirms that business need not be a battleground between ethics and economics, but can instead be a canvas for integration. It offers founders a structure within which they can grow without forgetting why they started. It reminds us that purpose is not something we perform for customers or funders—it is something we embed, honour, and evolve.

By grounding vision in structure, and structure in purpose, the blueprint transforms how we build. It transforms who we become. And it sets a new standard for what business can be: not just profitable, not just impactful, but deeply and enduringly aligned with the future we seek to create.

Chapter 8
Scaling Impact, Not Just Income

"Scaling." It's the buzzword that echoes through every startup incubator, investor pitch, and strategy offsite. It tends to conjure images of hypergrowth—rapid expansion, bigger numbers, more everything. But for mission-led entrepreneurs, that conventional vision raises a set of uncomfortable, often unspoken, questions. Can you really grow without eroding your principles? Is it possible to increase reach without trading away the intimacy, integrity, or nuance that gave your work its soul to begin with? And—more provocatively—what does success look like when your bottom line includes not only profit, but purpose, social impact, and emotional resonance?

Chapter 8 opens by asking us to reimagine scale entirely. Not as a mechanical exercise in duplication, but as a process of amplification—of values, of influence, of positive disruption. Scaling, in this context, isn't about churning out replicas of your product or service. It's about extending your mission's reach, deepening its roots, and ensuring its benefits reverberate far beyond your immediate sphere. Put differently, this is growth not as extraction, but as contribution.

The ripple effect, as metaphors go, feels apt. When purpose and profit are tethered—when a founder intentionally aligns financial success with something greater—the resulting waves touch everything. Supply chains, hiring standards, messaging, partnerships, public perception. And beyond the operational? Culture shifts. Expectations move. Industries get nudged. One regenerative agriculture business that introduces profit-sharing and carbon-negative methods doesn't just build a better farm—it sets a precedent. Suddenly, others look at what's possible through a new lens. And if done well, they follow.

Take Warby Parker. What began as a seemingly straightforward buy-one-give-one eyewear company became, quietly but powerfully, a cultural intervention. Their model wove social mission into the very architecture of the business. Not as a philanthropic afterthought, but as a defining logic. Today, their influence stretches well beyond retail. The founders now shape educational policy and civic projects—proof that when a business leads with values, its impact can exceed its category.

But such influence isn't conjured by vision alone. It requires growth with integrity. Many mission-led ventures are born in the singular voice of a founder—a therapist developing a trauma-informed coaching practice, say, or a craftsman building an ethical goods brand. At the outset, their presence is the brand. Their convictions pulse through every decision. But what happens when demand increases? When a mailing list swells, or media attention turns up the heat? At some point, it becomes impossible to do it all yourself—and scaling begins in earnest.

This juncture brings with it a host of internal shifts. Psychologically, structurally, even philosophically. The founder must evolve—from being the primary deliverer of value to becoming the custodian of values. This isn't just semantics. It's the difference between growing a business and building a movement. Suddenly, hiring isn't just about filling roles; it's about cultural transference. Delegating isn't merely a logistical relief—it's a litmus test of clarity. Because if your team doesn't know what the mission *is*, they certainly won't help extend it.

Therein lies the risk: the founder bottleneck. Growth stalls not because the market isn't there, but because the founder hasn't—or won't—let go. And yet, letting go without intentional frameworks is perilous. You can't scale purpose on vibes alone. At this point, systems become sacred.

Look, for instance, at Patagonia. The decision by its founder, Yvon Chouinard, to place ownership into a climate-focused trust wasn't a marketing manoeuvre. It was structural, enduring, and mission-bound. It created a legacy structure designed to outlast him—and continue serving the Earth. This is scaling with a clear philosophical spine. Not an exit strategy, but an anchoring one.

Still, growth often has a way of smuggling in compromises. So the essential question, one that should be asked not once but often, is this: *Would I still be doing this if the money were no longer part of the equation?* It's a difficult question—purposefully so. It's the question that wades through the spreadsheet sheen and tests the soul of the enterprise. Because over time, even well-meaning entrepreneurs can drift. The mission that once kept them up at night becomes a marketing line; the original "why" dissolves into operational routines and quarterly targets.

Which is precisely why this chapter advocates for regular recalibrations—mission audits, if you will. Intervals of inquiry. Is this decision still aligned with what I believe? Is this investor relationship serving the long-term vision or eroding it quietly? Does this product extension reflect our values—or merely our ambition? These aren't easy questions. They shouldn't be. But they're necessary if scaling is to remain a continuation of purpose rather than a departure from it.

To ground all this reflection in action, the chapter offers a 90-day plan: "Turning Purpose Into Profit Today." It's not a hustle blueprint. No "tenx" nonsense here. Rather, it's a focused invitation to choose one or two actions—no more—that realign your operations with your original mission. You might reconsider your pricing model to better honour the value you create. Or perhaps you revise your investor pitch, leading with purpose, not relegating it to the final slide. Maybe it's introducing a new key performance indicator that tracks not just income but impact. Small moves, yes—but done with consistency, they redirect the flow of growth.

What's often overlooked is that the most resilient mission-driven enterprises are not always the biggest or most visible. They're the ones that endure because they don't compromise the essence of their work. They navigate complexity without losing themselves. They understand that scaling isn't about dominance—it's about deepening. And deepening, it turns out, is where real influence lives.

There's no illusion here. This process is hard. Scaling with integrity is not a frictionless climb—it's a thousand trade-offs, some of them painful. It asks for rigour of thought and heart. But it also unlocks a rare form of success—one that's not just measured in reach or valuation, but in the quiet confidence that you built something worthy. Something that matters.

So this is where the book leaves you: with the provocation that mission-driven money is not a fringe experiment. It is, arguably, the future—an evolving template for how wealth might function in a time of ecological urgency and social rebalancing. It invites entrepreneurs to grow not in defiance of the world's needs, but in response to them. To lead with humility, build with discernment, and scale with conscience.

If enough of us accept that invitation, the shape of business might shift altogether. The scoreboard may no longer be defined solely by accumulation. Instead, we might begin to measure our worth by the quality of our contribution—and the resonance of the ripples we leave behind.

The Ripple Effect: How Mission-Driven Success Creates Generational Change

The dominant narratives around wealth have long centred on individual success—net worth, personal achievement, prestige. In this narrow framing, wealth is static, inherited or accumulated, often hoarded, and usually isolated from any meaningful sense of collective responsibility. But for mission-driven entrepreneurs, wealth is increasingly being redefined—not as an end state, but as a catalyst. When aligned with purpose, financial success becomes less about personal security and more about systemic transformation. This shift marks a quiet revolution, one that ripples outward—through families, communities, industries, and ultimately, generations.

At the heart of this ripple effect is the understanding that money is not value-neutral. It is a mechanism of power—capable of reinforcing existing hierarchies or dismantling them. Mission-driven wealth actively chooses the latter. It seeks to redirect the flow of capital toward social equity, environmental sustainability, cultural preservation, and generational healing. Unlike traditional philanthropic models that tend to operate after wealth has been accumulated—often as an exercise in legacy management—mission-aligned capital embeds impact at the source. It bakes justice and purpose into the way money is made, not just how it is spent.

This distinction is vital. When wealth creation itself is infused with ethics, transparency, and intentionality, its benefits transcend the immediate bottom line. It empowers new models of entrepreneurship that are inclusive, restorative, and intergenerational by design. It challenges extractive economics and introduces a new metric of success—*what happens to the people and systems that intersect with your prosperity?*

Consider the story of Fawn Weaver, founder and CEO of Uncle Nearest Premium Whiskey. The brand was launched not just to sell a product, but to rewrite history—specifically, the overlooked legacy of Nathan "Nearest" Green, the formerly enslaved man who taught Jack Daniel the art of distilling. Weaver's mission was not merely commercial; it was reparative. She used the company's profits to fund college scholarships for Green's descendants, invest in Black-owned businesses, and expand economic opportunities within historically marginalised communities. Her approach to business is not an act of charity—it is a model of structurally embedded justice. The wealth she is building is not isolated in shareholders' accounts; it is actively dismantling generational disenfranchisement and rewriting narratives.

Such examples highlight a powerful insight: when entrepreneurs consciously design their wealth-building mechanisms to benefit others, the ripple effect becomes exponential. Children grow up witnessing models of ethical leadership. Communities experience direct material uplift. Industries shift their standards. In some cases, entirely new economies emerge. Social entrepreneur Muhammad Yunus, founder of Grameen Bank, famously demonstrated this through microfinance. By providing small loans to impoverished women in Bangladesh, he didn't just create a bank—he seeded a global movement that challenged traditional banking models and empowered millions. The ripple of his initial idea has touched countless lives, not through charity, but through a reimagination of economic agency.

At a family level, the impact of mission-driven wealth is equally profound. Children raised in households where values are integrated into enterprise—where decisions are explained through both ethical and financial lenses—are more likely to develop a healthy, empowered relationship with money. They learn that financial resources can be tools for liberation, not merely instruments of status or stress. They see wealth not as something to display, but something to direct. And crucially, they inherit not only assets, but *a philosophy*—a way of thinking about contribution, power, and responsibility.

This is particularly important in communities where historical access to wealth has been limited. For first-generation wealth creators, aligning purpose with financial growth can disrupt long-standing cycles of scarcity and exclusion. When these individuals reinvest in education, health, or local entrepreneurship, they become force multipliers—creating ecosystems where others can also thrive. Their success is not seen as exceptionalism, but as precedent.

One need look no further than the impact of Arlan Hamilton, the founder of Backstage Capital, which invests in underestimated founders—women, people of colour, and LGBTQ+ entrepreneurs. Hamilton's personal story is remarkable: she was homeless while building her venture fund, driven by a mission to diversify the startup ecosystem. But the generational impact of her work is even more compelling. By injecting capital into communities that have historically been sidelined, she is not only creating opportunities in the present—she is setting the stage for a new generation of investors, founders, and changemakers who will carry that torch forward. The wealth she creates is circular, not linear. And its ripple will long outlast her tenure.

These case studies reveal that mission-aligned wealth is not about dilution of profit, but deepening of purpose. In fact, the businesses that succeed most sustainably tend to be those that are rooted in a strong sense of mission. Customers trust them. Employees stay longer. Partners align more easily. Resilience is stronger. And while the returns may not always be immediate, they are durable—financially and socially.

There is, however, a critical caveat. The ripple effect is not automatic. It must be designed. Entrepreneurs must be intentional not only in their personal conduct but in the structures they build. This means interrogating every layer of the enterprise: supply chains, governance models, incentive structures, succession plans. It means asking uncomfortable questions: Who benefits from my growth? Whose labour or land am I leveraging? What does wealth look like in my industry, and how do I subvert the parts of that image that are extractive or exclusionary?

Such interrogation can be confronting. It often reveals inherited assumptions and silent complicities. But it is also liberating. It opens the door to new forms of entrepreneurship—cooperatives, B Corps, mutual aid models—that decouple financial growth from systemic harm. It also fosters humility. Mission-driven entrepreneurs who understand their place in a wider ecosystem are less likely to centre themselves and more likely to build collaboratively. Their ripple is not about personal branding—it is about shared transformation.

This perspective also transforms the way success is measured. Traditional metrics—revenue, EBITDA, user growth—remain relevant. But they are accompanied by qualitative indicators: levels of community trust, rates of internal equity, impact on environmental regeneration, feedback from those most affected by your business. These are not soft metrics. They are the true test of legacy.

And legacy, in the context of mission-driven entrepreneurship, is not a monument to the founder. It is a momentum that continues beyond them. It is the scholarship fund that renews every year, the company culture that outlives its architect, the community that thrives long after the press release fades. It is the grandmother who uses her baking business to fund girls' education, and whose granddaughters go on to start tech companies rooted in equity. It is the designer who champions sustainable fashion and influences a whole generation of consumers to think differently about what they wear. These are not ripples—they are tides.

In a world increasingly defined by volatility and inequality, the opportunity—and responsibility—of mission-driven entrepreneurs is immense. They are not just building products or platforms. They are shaping the ethical architecture of future economies. Their choices today will define what wealth means tomorrow. Will it continue to concentrate? Or will it circulate? Will it build fortresses? Or will it build futures?

The ripple effect of mission-aligned success is perhaps the most powerful lever we have for lasting change. It proves that entrepreneurship need not be extractive to be effective. That wealth need not be hoarded to be generational. And that impact is not a side effect—it is the substance. When money meets meaning, when ambition meets ethics, and when purpose is embedded in every financial decision, the results echo far beyond balance sheets.

They echo through families. Through institutions. Through time. And they remind us that the truest form of legacy is not what we leave behind—but what we set in motion.

From Solopreneur to Movement Leader: Expanding Your Influence

The solopreneur is a powerful figure in modern business mythology—scrappy, agile, deeply committed to a cause, and intimately connected to every detail of their enterprise. Many mission-driven ventures begin this way, with a single founder wearing every hat, from creative visionary to customer service lead. There is immense power in this phase: decisions are made quickly, brand voice is authentic, and every touchpoint carries the DNA of the founder's values. But there comes a point where the limitations of a one-person operation become obvious. Demand increases, systems strain, and the reach of the business plateaus—not because the mission has lost relevance, but because the infrastructure cannot support expansion.

This moment presents a pivotal decision. Some founders double down on doing more with less, leading to burnout or stagnation. Others scale reactively, outsourcing core functions and diluting the ethos that made their work distinctive. But a third path exists—one that requires deliberate transformation from solopreneur to *movement leader*. This evolution is not about ego or empire-building. It is about building capacity for impact without compromising authenticity.

At the heart of this transition lies a subtle shift in mindset: from doing *everything yourself* to becoming the steward of a cause larger than yourself. Movement leaders don't just sell products or services; they catalyse conversations, reshape industries, and invite others into a shared purpose. They stop being the sole protagonist in their business narrative and begin to serve as facilitators of a collective mission. This transition requires strategic thinking, emotional resilience, and a profound trust in others.

One of the most critical early decisions in this shift is identifying *what to hold onto* and *what to release*. Not every function needs to be centralised in the founder. Tasks like bookkeeping, customer service, or social media scheduling can often be systematised or delegated without loss of integrity. But there are core aspects—vision, voice, values—that must remain closely guarded, especially during early stages of scale. Authenticity is not maintained by doing everything yourself; it is preserved by ensuring that those who join the team deeply understand and embody the mission.

A strong example of this principle in action is seen in the evolution of Tabitha Brown, an American actress turned vegan lifestyle entrepreneur. Her personal brand was initially built on unscripted, heartfelt videos filmed in her kitchen. As her influence grew, she expanded into cookbooks, children's programming, wellness products, and even a fashion line—all while maintaining her authentic voice. How? By being deeply selective about partnerships, insisting on creative control where it mattered, and bringing on team members who understood not only the business but the heart behind it. Her transition from solopreneur to movement leader was not defined by scale alone, but by her ability to scale *alignment*.

Another central task for movement leaders is defining a *scalable version of trust.* When businesses grow, the founder can no longer personally connect with every customer, client, or stakeholder. This introduces a challenge: how do you maintain the intimacy and credibility of the solopreneur era at scale? The answer lies in institutionalising values—not just in a mission statement, but in hiring practices, operational procedures, and decision-making frameworks. It's about creating culture by design, not default.

The global cosmetics company Lush exemplifies this well. Known for its ethical sourcing, cruelty-free products, and political activism, Lush has managed to grow into a multinational brand while retaining grassroots credibility. This is not accidental. They build transparency into their supply chains, empower local store managers to engage in community activism, and ensure that internal processes reinforce, rather than erode, their stated values. Leadership is decentralised, but the mission is centralised—anchored by systems that incentivise integrity over expediency.

For founders seeking to make this transition, one practical exercise involves mapping their current business onto a framework of *roles vs. responsibilities.* What are you currently doing that someone else could do just as well—or better? What functions are uniquely yours because they embody your voice, your story, or your strategic vision? From there, begin to prototype a support system. This doesn't necessarily mean hiring a full-time team on day one. It could start with strategic contractors, part-time collaborators, or co-creators who share your purpose and bring complementary skills. The goal is to gradually shift from a solo act to an ensemble—without losing the coherence that made your solo performance compelling.

Importantly, expanding your influence as a movement leader requires reframing your relationship to visibility. Many solopreneurs build their brand around personal charisma or expertise. While this is a powerful way to build trust, it can become a bottleneck if every growth initiative depends on your presence. Movement leaders create frameworks that outlive their own spotlight. They spotlight *the work* instead of merely *themselves.* They amplify team members, community stories, and ecosystem partners—not out of humility alone, but because they understand that sustainable influence is *distributed influence.*

This principle is evident in the work of Amanda Nguyen, the founder of Rise, a civil rights organisation focused on protecting the rights of sexual assault survivors. Nguyen began as a passionate advocate sharing her personal story. But as Rise grew into a global movement influencing policy change in multiple countries, Nguyen expanded her role from storyteller to strategist, training other survivors to become legislative advocates. Her influence multiplied not because she spoke louder, but because she equipped others to speak for themselves.

Leadership at this stage also requires grappling with the tension between *growth and governance.* As you expand your platform, how do you ensure that your operations, legal structures, and financial models support—not constrain—your mission? Some founders transition from sole proprietorships to social enterprises, cooperatives, or even non-profit hybrids to better reflect their evolving goals. These decisions should not be made lightly. But they offer an opportunity to encode your values structurally, ensuring that your influence is not dependent on good intentions alone.

Ultimately, the evolution from solopreneur to movement leader is not just a career transition—it is a personal metamorphosis. It involves letting go of control while holding tightly to clarity. It demands a new relationship with power—less about individual will, more about collective momentum. It invites a wider definition of success: not just what you can build, but what you can inspire; not just what you can execute, but what you can *enable.*

The most effective movement leaders do not position themselves as saviours or gurus. They position themselves as *hosts*—curating spaces, conversations, and systems where others can grow, lead, and innovate. They are not the sole authors of change, but its most faithful stewards.

This chapter invites you to see yourself not as the ceiling of your enterprise, but as its foundation. Not as the irreplaceable centre, but as the irrefutable spark. The question is not merely how far you can go, but how wide you can reach without losing the essence of why you began. Scale is not the antithesis of authenticity. With the right strategy and a grounded sense of purpose, it can be its amplifier.

You are not just building a business. You are shaping a movement. And that movement begins not with louder declarations, but with quieter, deeper alignment—between your vision, your systems, and the world you are working to create.

The Ultimate Test: Would You Still Do This Without Money?

Every mission-driven entrepreneur, at some point in their growth, encounters a piercing moment of truth—a question that cuts through strategy decks, performance metrics, and financial forecasts. That question is not about scalability or valuation. It is about *conviction*: Would you still do this work if it never made you rich? Would you still build this business, teach this idea, serve this community—if there were no guarantee of a financial windfall? In a culture that so readily conflates profit with purpose, asking this question is a profound act of reorientation. It shifts the spotlight from outcomes to origins, from what you stand to gain to *what you stand for.*

At first glance, the question may appear purely philosophical. But it has deeply practical consequences. Understanding whether your mission can withstand the absence of money is not about martyrdom or romantic idealism. It is about testing the structural integrity of your motivation. In the volatile landscape of entrepreneurship—especially the purpose-led kind—there will be seasons where returns are slow, where growth is erratic, where your energy exceeds your earnings. If your drive is tethered too tightly to the promise of financial success, your resilience may fray. But if your mission is anchored in something deeper, more intrinsic, it becomes its own source of fuel.

This is not to suggest that financial success is unimportant. Quite the opposite: mission-driven businesses must be economically sustainable to endure and to scale their impact. Yet, clarifying whether the *desire* for money is guiding your purpose—or whether money is simply the tool that allows that purpose to flourish—is essential. It changes the way you design your business, relate to your customers, and assess opportunities. It even affects how you recover from failure.

Consider the case of Blake Mycoskie, founder of TOMS Shoes. His business model—buy one, give one—was lauded for blending commercial success with philanthropic intent. But as the company scaled and critics questioned the long-term efficacy of shoe donations, Mycoskie returned to a deeper interrogation of his motivations. Was he building a global brand—or leading a movement to alleviate poverty? That distinction prompted a re-evaluation of the company's impact model, shifting from giveaways to more sustainable, community-driven development projects. Had profit been the sole motivator, such a pivot might not have occurred. But the deeper mission—with or without its original business model—remained intact.

True motivation reveals itself not in moments of reward, but in moments of ambiguity. When results stall, when acclaim fades, when momentum slows—what compels you to keep showing up? The answer to this question can reveal whether you are driven by validation or by vocation. Entrepreneurs who remain committed even when external rewards wane are those whose work is intrinsically meaningful. They are not chasing a payday. They are answering a calling.

This calling, however, need not be grandiose. It need not invoke universal language of justice or transformation. For some, it may be the quiet commitment to craftsmanship, or the joy of creating beautiful things that make life easier, healthier, or more dignified. The real test is whether the work itself carries meaning, even when the revenue does not reflect the effort. This is not a call to martyrdom. It is an invitation to ask: If my business failed tomorrow, would I still care about this problem? Would I find another way to address it, write about it, advocate for it?

The inverse of this question is also worth asking: If someone offered you vast sums of money to walk away from your mission and do something completely different—would you take it? Many entrepreneurs believe they are mission-driven until a more lucrative, less aligned opportunity emerges. Here again, clarity of motivation becomes your compass. If you would abandon your cause for convenience or cash, then your mission may not be a mission at all. It may be a tactic—a socially acceptable wrapper for a personal ambition.

This test is especially important for those whose brands are built around their personal identity. In the age of the influencer-entrepreneur, where visibility and profitability often go hand-in-hand, it's easy to conflate purpose with persona. But personal branding, however compelling, is not the same as purpose. One can fade quickly. The other endures. Entrepreneurs like Jamila Jamil, who launched the I Weigh movement to challenge beauty norms and promote radical inclusivity, have demonstrated that even if the mainstream platform disappears, the mission can find new life through advocacy, writing, or community building. The medium may change—but the motivation does not.

This distinction is also crucial when raising capital or entering partnerships. Investors and collaborators will inevitably ask about revenue, growth, and exit strategy. But discerning, values-aligned stakeholders will also look for signals of genuine commitment. They want to know that you're not just trend-surfing or impact-washing. They want to know that your belief in your work runs deeper than the funding cycle. Being able to say, with integrity, "This matters to me whether it scales or not," is not just noble. It's persuasive. It builds trust.

Practically speaking, exploring this question can also help refine your business model. If you would still do your work without the promise of profit, where would you do it? How would you fund it? Who would you serve? These questions can reveal whether your current model supports or distorts your mission. For example, a wellness coach driven by a desire to make mental health support accessible might realise that her high-ticket offerings, while profitable, are excluding the very audience she hoped to reach.

That insight might lead her to introduce a tiered pricing model, develop open-access content, or seek grants to subsidise care. Again, the mission doesn't disappear—it simply finds new channels.

Some of the most transformative movements in history began not with capital, but with conviction. Think of Wangari Maathai's Green Belt Movement, which empowered Kenyan women to plant millions of trees and fight deforestation. Her work began with a few seedlings and a belief in environmental justice. There were no venture rounds or scalability reports—just persistence, community, and vision. Over time, the resources followed. But they did not *define* the mission. They supported it.

The question, "Would you still do this without money?" is ultimately about *alignment.* It forces a reconciliation between inner and outer motivations. If the answer is yes, then your path is likely resilient, adaptable, and meaningful—even if it evolves. If the answer is no, then it's worth examining whether your work is truly purpose-led—or merely profit-driven dressed in purpose language.

Of course, this reflection must be balanced with the reality that mission without means is not sustainable. You must eat, rest, pay staff, and grow. The goal is not to abandon financial ambition. It is to *right-size* it—to situate it within a larger ecosystem of meaning. Money should be the consequence of doing work that matters, not the sole reason for doing it.

As you continue to grow your mission-driven enterprise, keep this question close. Let it shape your hiring, your pricing, your messaging. Let it temper your ambitions when they drift toward vanity metrics. Let it console you when the revenue dips and you wonder whether it's all worth it. Because if your answer remains yes—yes, I would do this anyway—then you're not just building a business. You're building something much rarer: a legacy that outlasts the market cycle.

And that is the ultimate test—not only of your motivation, but of your movement.

Your Next 90 Days: Turning Purpose Into Profit Today

The intellectual appeal of purpose-driven entrepreneurship is undeniable. It allows founders to weave meaning into their work, align enterprise with values, and resist the empty acceleration of hustle culture. But inspiration without implementation is insufficient. Purpose must not only feel compelling—it must function. The transition from philosophy to practicality is where most mission-led businesses either build momentum or stall. The next 90 days, then, become a proving ground. Not for perfection, but for *alignment in motion.* It is where vision meets velocity.

Turning purpose into profit begins with a redefinition of what profit *is.* This does not imply a rejection of financial returns. Rather, it calls for a recalibration: profit is no longer the sole metric of success, but one measure among many. Others may include deepened impact, increased visibility, improved well-being for the entrepreneur and team, or greater community engagement. The distinction is subtle but critical—by widening the aperture, we allow for a more integrated approach to growth. From this vantage point, financial profit is not an accidental by-product of doing good, nor a betrayal of ethics. It is a fuel source, a form of energy, a tool for expansion.

The first step in the 90-day window is diagnostic. Before introducing new initiatives or chasing metrics, founders must take stock of where their business currently sits on the alignment spectrum. This includes an honest assessment of revenue models, operational processes, partnerships, messaging, and product or service offerings. Are they consistent with your values? Do they reflect your stated mission? Are there areas of drift—decisions that were once made for survival but are now out of sync with where you want to go?

This diagnostic phase is not a luxury—it is an imperative. When done well, it can expose the "invisible compromises" that quietly undermine authenticity. For example, a sustainability-focused skincare brand might discover that their packaging choices, though cost-effective, rely on unsustainable plastics. Or a coaching business committed to accessibility might recognise that their pricing model inadvertently excludes the very audience they wish to serve. These are not failures. They are friction points—places where purpose and profit are not yet in full conversation. Identifying them allows for corrective strategy that does not sacrifice growth, but deepens coherence.

Once the business has been honestly mapped, the next step is prioritisation. Founders are notoriously good at generating ideas and poor at sequencing them. Over the next 90 days, the goal is not to *do everything*. It is to focus on the one or two actions that will generate the greatest return—not just financially, but in terms of integrity, clarity, and momentum. For some, this might mean launching a purpose-aligned product line or service. For others, it might involve refining the brand narrative to better communicate mission to customers and investors. Still others may need to redesign internal systems—team structures, workflows, or cultural rituals—to reflect shared values.

Take the example of the British social enterprise Too Good To Go, which tackles food waste by connecting consumers with surplus food from restaurants and shops. Its initial success stemmed not from trying to solve every problem in the food system, but from executing a single, purpose-aligned intervention with clarity. By staying disciplined in their offering, they built traction, trust, and eventually, revenue. Over time, they scaled, added features, and expanded geographies—but only after anchoring themselves in a sharply defined impact.

For solopreneurs or micro-teams, the next 90 days should also involve building systems that support sustainability—not just in terms of growth, but in human energy. Burnout remains one of the greatest risks to purpose-led entrepreneurs. Passion, when not paired with strategic pacing, leads to depletion. A founder may love their work, but without boundaries, rest, and recovery, they risk collapsing the very mission they are trying to uphold. Thus, part of the action plan must include operational discipline: time-blocking for deep work, outsourcing low-impact tasks, building in non-negotiable breaks. These are not indulgences. They are investments in long-term resilience.

From a financial perspective, the next 90 days are also a powerful window for testing pricing models. Too often, purpose-driven founders undercharge in the name of accessibility or humility. But underpricing is not virtuous—it is unsustainable. If the business cannot support the founder, the team, or the broader impact goals, it will eventually implode. Testing new pricing strategies—whether through tiered offerings, bundled services, or value-based pricing—allows the founder to observe customer response, measure retention, and adjust with integrity. Crucially, this is not about extracting maximum value from customers. It is about ensuring that the value *you deliver* is matched by the value *you receive.*

One useful case study here is The Female Lead, a non-profit media platform that promotes women's stories. Initially grant-funded, the organisation shifted toward a blended revenue model that includes sponsored content, educational licensing, and digital courses. This transition was not driven by greed, but by a recognition that reliance on donor funding limited their autonomy and ability to plan long-term. By monetising with alignment, they expanded reach *and* impact—proof that purpose and commercial strategy are not incompatible, but complementary when thoughtfully designed.

During this implementation phase, it is also essential to return to storytelling. Mission-driven businesses thrive on narrative. Over the next 90 days, rearticulate your story—not as a static pitch deck or a homepage blurb, but as a living narrative that evolves with your business. What problem are you solving? Why does it matter? Who are you serving? How does your solution connect to something larger than commerce? Crafting this story will not only refine your marketing, but will clarify your own sense of why this work is worth doing. Done well, it becomes a beacon for collaborators, customers, and capital.

This period should also include reflection checkpoints—moments where progress is assessed not only in terms of tasks completed, but in terms of *alignment deepened.* These moments should ask: Am I still clear on my mission? Is my revenue growing in ways that reinforce, rather than compromise, my values? What am I learning about my customers, my team, and myself? Reflection, in this context, is not passive. It is the engine of iteration.

Looking ahead, the next 90 days are not a standalone sprint. They are the first of many chapters in a longer narrative. But they are disproportionately important. Because in this window, habits are formed, systems are built, and confidence is either earned or eroded. For mission-led founders, confidence does not come from bravado. It comes from *evidence*—seeing that your ideas, when operationalised, actually work. That people respond. That money flows. That the mission *moves.*

There is no one-size-fits-all blueprint. But there is a universal imperative: act. Do not wait for perfection. Do not wait for the entire map. Move with the information you have. Test your assumptions. Talk to your customers. Raise your prices if they're too low. Say no to partnerships that dilute your vision. Refine your offer so that it resonates more clearly. And above all, *build systems that reflect your purpose*, not merely your ambition.

This is what it means to turn purpose into profit—not by abandoning one for the other, but by creating a structure in which they reinforce one another. Profit, when aligned with purpose, is not a compromise. It is a consequence—a natural outcome of clarity, courage, and consistent value creation.

Over the next 90 days, your task is not to complete the mission, but to embody it. To begin building the world your purpose envisions, one decision at a time. To prove—to yourself first, and then to others—that purpose is not the antithesis of profit. It is its most powerful engine.

Let this be the season where your values leave the page and enter the process. Where your vision becomes your structure. And where your work becomes not just viable—but vital.

Final Thought: Mission-Driven Money as the Future of Wealth

For generations, wealth has been narrowly defined. It has been measured in currency, accumulated assets, and comparative advantage. The dominant narrative told us that success was a solitary pursuit, validated by financial gains and public recognition. But this definition—though persistent—is rapidly becoming obsolete. Across industries, cultures, and demographics, a new paradigm is emerging: one where purpose, impact, and human flourishing are not footnotes to profit, but core components of what it means to be truly wealthy.

This redefinition of wealth is not a sentimental turn away from economic competence. It is a pragmatic evolution. In an increasingly interconnected, conscious, and crisis-aware world, businesses that ignore meaning are not just morally misaligned—they are strategically vulnerable. Stakeholders—whether customers, employees, or investors—are no longer content to participate in enterprises that extract value at the expense of ethics. They are looking for alignment, for coherence between what a company says and what it does, for leaders who don't just perform virtue but practice it in their decision-making.

Mission-driven money is not an abstract theory. It is a growing force, evidenced by the exponential rise of impact investing, benefit corporations, ethical consumerism, and regenerative business practices. According to the Global Impact Investing Network, the impact investment market surpassed $1.1 trillion in assets under management in 2022, a figure that not only underscores investor interest, but reflects a broader societal shift. People are asking more nuanced questions about where their money goes, what it supports, and what legacy it leaves. Increasingly, they are recognising that every pound, dollar, or rupee is a vote—for the kind of world we want to build.

Consider the story of Yvon Chouinard, the founder of Patagonia. In 2022, he transferred ownership of his multi-billion-dollar company to a trust and nonprofit dedicated to fighting climate change. This was not a publicity stunt. It was a radical act of structural integrity. Chouinard reimagined wealth not as a personal inheritance, but as a vehicle for planetary stewardship. He decoupled success from personal enrichment and recoupled it with responsibility. His decision sent ripples through the business community, challenging even the most progressive companies to examine the depth of their commitments.

But mission-driven money is not just the domain of billionaires. It plays out just as powerfully in the decisions of small business owners who choose to pay living wages, of freelancers who refuse exploitative contracts, of educators who create accessible platforms despite commercial pressure to monetise every interaction. It lives in the micro-decisions: in choosing transparency over expediency, community over competition, long-term value over short-term gain.

These choices may not always produce immediate financial windfalls. But they do generate *trust*, and in the economy of the future, trust is the most valuable currency. Trust builds brand loyalty, attracts aligned collaborators, and fosters resilience in volatile markets. Companies that consistently honour their mission develop reputational capital that no marketing budget can buy. They endure not because they are the cheapest or the fastest, but because they are the *most trusted.*

The shift toward mission-driven wealth also invites a deeper personal reckoning. What does it mean to be rich? Is it surplus or sufficiency? Is it control or contribution? Is it accumulation or activation? For many entrepreneurs, particularly those from historically marginalised communities, the traditional wealth narrative was never accessible or aspirational. Rewriting it is not just a matter of preference—it is an act of liberation. It allows individuals to pursue financial empowerment without abandoning cultural integrity, community ties, or ancestral wisdom.

Take, for example, the growing number of Indigenous-led enterprises that are reinterpreting business through the lens of relational economics. These ventures often prioritise reciprocity, ecological balance, and intergenerational responsibility over extractive models of growth. They remind us that money, when unmoored from moral frameworks, becomes a disorienting force. But when anchored in meaning, it becomes a generative tool—one that honours lineage while shaping legacy.

This is not to romanticise the road. Choosing to align your finances with your values is often harder, slower, and more complex than defaulting to conventional paradigms. It requires courage, clarity, and sometimes sacrifice. But it also yields a different kind of wealth—a sense of coherence between who you are and what you do. A sense that your business is not simply a transaction engine, but a vehicle for transformation.

And this coherence matters. Because in the long arc of entrepreneurial life, it is not the quarters of peak profit that define you. It is the cumulative integrity of your decisions. Did you build something that healed, or harmed? Did you create conditions for others to thrive? Did your work reflect your principles when no one was watching?

In a world facing escalating inequality, ecological degradation, and widespread disillusionment, the stakes are too high to build businesses that do not serve a broader good. The future of wealth must be regenerative, not extractive. It must be relational, not individualistic. It must be accountable, not insulated. Mission-driven money is not a passing trend—it is a recalibration of what it means to be successful in a fragile and interdependent world.

This redefinition requires us to update not only our business plans, but our personal beliefs. We must interrogate the scripts we have inherited about success, worth, and ambition. We must release the idea that doing good and doing well exist in separate spheres. They do not. In fact, the most enduring wealth—the kind that outlives us—is precisely the kind that nourishes others while sustaining us.

So as you close this book, the invitation is not merely to adopt new strategies or frameworks. It is to adopt a new *philosophy*—one that treats money as a means, not an end. One that centres meaning, even as it builds markets. One that understands that the future of wealth is not found in escaping the world, but in engaging it fully—with conscience, creativity, and care.

You do not need to be perfect. You do not need to have all the answers. But you must begin. Begin with the truth of your mission. Begin with the courage to act on it. Begin with the quiet insistence that wealth without purpose is not wealth at all—it is simply accumulation. And accumulation, without direction, does not lead to freedom. But when money is mission-aligned—when it flows through you and not merely to you—it becomes something else entirely.

It becomes legacy. It becomes movement. It becomes a future worth building.

Conclusion
What Makes This Book Unique?

For as long as there have been books on money, most have adhered to a familiar playbook: earn diligently, spend cautiously, invest wisely, and if all goes to plan—retire early with a satisfied smile. Some offered steps, others spun philosophies, a rare few changed the trajectory of their readers' lives. Yet surprisingly few paused to ask a more essential question: *Why* do you want wealth in the first place? What kind of life are you hoping that wealth will enable—or protect? That, right there, is the blind spot this book was written to illuminate. Not simply another how-to on business growth, nor just a meditation on purpose, but something more integrated—a weaving of science and soul, urging a reevaluation of what financial success truly means.

What sets this work apart is the breadth of its foundation. It doesn't rely on advice through the narrow lens of business strategy, nor does it peddle recycled maxims from the well-trodden world of self-improvement. Instead, it draws on a rich blend of neuroscience, psychology, and behavioural economics to unpack why some entrepreneurs thrive with lasting fulfilment while others flame out—sometimes spectacularly. But the science here isn't just ornamental. It's practical. Clarifying. Consider the role of dopamine in driving motivation: when left unchecked, it fuels the chase for ever-higher financial highs, yet rarely delivers satisfaction. Or the notion of scarcity thinking, rooted in early developmental psychology—how childhood beliefs about safety and worth can warp adult choices around pricing, partnerships, even risk appetite. These aren't just interesting theories; they're tools. And in the right hands, they reshape both business strategy and personal wellbeing.

Grounding these ideas are real-world accounts from entrepreneurs who've faced the frictions of purpose and profit head-on. Their stories aren't scrubbed clean or optimised for retrospective glory. They're raw, honest, at times contradictory—because that's how growth often looks in the trenches. We meet founders who built things they no longer believed in, only to dismantle and rebuild with deeper intent. The range is deliberate. Regenerative agriculture, SaaS platforms, social ventures, artisanal products—you'll find no single prototype here. Just a shared thread: people striving to build enterprises that reflect who they are, not just what they can monetise.

And it's precisely this multiplicity that challenges an old, persistent myth—that mission-led businesses are somehow less serious, less scalable, or less disciplined than their traditional counterparts. On the contrary. As these examples consistently show, aligning your values with your operations takes *more*—not less—rigour. It demands clearer strategy, deeper emotional fluency, and a willingness to play a longer game. You don't just lead with a plan; you lead with presence. With a sense of legacy that isn't about what you leave behind, but what you *set in motion.*

Another layer to this book's structure—one that quietly repositions its intent—is its interactivity. This is not a text to passively consume and shelve. It's designed to provoke action. Throughout, you'll find frameworks and tools intended to close the distance between knowing and doing. The Mission-Mapping Blueprint. The Burnout Barometer. The Values Compass. They're not filler, and they're certainly not academic exercises. They're practical instruments, crafted to shift you from insight to execution. Because let's be honest—information, on its own, is inert. And purpose, without systems to sustain it, has a tendency to fray at the edges.

These tools aren't about imposing a fixed methodology, either. They're adaptable—rooted in behavioural science and coaching psychology, yes, but designed to flex with you. Writing a Money Mission Statement, for instance, isn't just about honing your elevator pitch. It's a deep alignment process, one that asks you to embed your values into every financial decision—pricing, hiring, investing, even messaging. When used well, these frameworks translate inner clarity into outward coherence.

At the heart of all this is a bold assertion: that rethinking wealth is no longer optional. It is, in fact, overdue. We're living in an era where the old metrics—maximum shareholder value, endless growth, relentless optimisation—are cracking under pressure.

Ecologically, economically, socially—the seams are showing. And so this book offers an alternative. Not an easier one, but a wiser one. A model that respects sustainability, equity, and human dignity as non-negotiables alongside profit. One that sees markets not as detached mechanisms, but as expressions of our collective values.

The hope here is to reposition the idea of wealth as something relational. Something regenerative. To break with the scarcity-driven myth of the lone winner and return to something more grounded: stewardship, interdependence, responsibility. Yes, you can build a profitable company without abandoning your ethics. Yes, influence can scale without your message thinning out. But only if you're vigilant—about what you're building, what you're compromising, and what you refuse to give away.

For those who have felt caught between the two extremes—traditional business guides that feel bloodless, and hyper-spiritual manifestos that gloss over hard trade-offs—this book aims to sit squarely in the middle. Grounded, but aspirational. Ambitious, but aligned. It's not anti-growth. It's just asking what you're growing *towards*.

So, if you've made it this far, it's fair to say the ideas have landed. You've read. You've reflected. And now? Now comes the part that actually matters. Action. Not sweeping gestures or overnight overhauls. Just small, decisive moves. Raise your rates if you've been underselling. Set one policy that better reflects your values. Decline that partnership that doesn't sit right. Choose *one* next step—and take it with intention. Because momentum built on coherence will, in the long run, outperform momentum built on compromise.

The businesses that endure—truly endure—will not be those that scale the fastest or make the loudest noise. They'll be the ones that stand for something solid. That embed care into their culture. That wield money as a tool for alignment, not as a proxy for worth.

And it's there, in that quiet, consistent alignment, where real wealth begins to take root. Where profit and peace are no longer at odds.

Where success isn't defined by optics, but by impact. Not simply by scale, but by substance.

That, in the end, is what this book hopes to offer—not a sharper strategy, but a deeper foundation. One that empowers you to step off the well-worn path of conventional success and craft a vision of wealth that is entirely your own.

Bridges Neuroscience, Psychology, and Behavioral Economics to Explain the Deep Connection Between Purpose and Financial Success

For too long, financial success has been treated as a mechanistic outcome: the result of spreadsheets, strategy, and scale. But the deeper truth, emerging across disciplines from neuroscience to behavioural economics, is that wealth creation is not purely rational. It is driven by human motivation—an alchemy of cognition, emotion, and meaning. When that motivation is tethered to a clear and compelling purpose, something profound happens: individuals become more resilient, decisions become more coherent, and value creation becomes more sustainable. This intersection of brain science, psychology, and economic behaviour is not just intellectually fascinating—it is the foundation for a new model of entrepreneurial success.

At the neural level, purpose functions as a stabilising and energising force. Research in affective neuroscience reveals that goal-directed behaviour engages the brain's reward circuitry, particularly the mesolimbic dopamine system. Dopamine, often mischaracterised as a simple "pleasure" chemical, is more accurately understood as a driver of *anticipation* and *persistence*. It is not triggered by passive enjoyment, but by the pursuit of meaningful goals. When entrepreneurs feel connected to a larger mission, their brains receive a continuous stream of motivational reinforcement. This neurological feedback loop increases focus, stamina, and adaptability—qualities essential for navigating the volatile terrain of business building.

But purpose does more than stimulate reward centres. It also modulates stress. Studies have shown that individuals with a strong sense of meaning in life exhibit lower cortisol levels, even under pressure. From a practical perspective, this translates to enhanced emotional regulation during high-stakes moments—negotiations, funding rounds, product pivots. Purpose, in this context, acts as a kind of biological buffer, protecting cognitive performance from the corrosive effects of anxiety. This is not abstract theory. It is a competitive advantage.

In parallel, psychology provides further insight into why mission-aligned entrepreneurship is uniquely potent. Self-Determination Theory (SDT), developed by Edward Deci and Richard Ryan, posits that human beings are most motivated when three core psychological needs are met: autonomy, competence, and relatedness. Traditional financial incentives often overlook these dimensions, focusing instead on external rewards. But when a business aligns with a founder's values and contributes to something larger than the self, all three needs are simultaneously fulfilled. The entrepreneur feels agency, mastery, and connection—conditions that lead to intrinsic motivation, which is both more enduring and more productive than extrinsic pressure.

This distinction between intrinsic and extrinsic drivers also has significant implications in behavioural economics. Scholars like Dan Ariely and Richard Thaler have demonstrated that people frequently make choices that defy traditional economic logic—not because they are irrational, but because they are responding to meaning, identity, and social context. Entrepreneurs, too, are not rational actors in the classical sense. They overinvest, take asymmetric risks, and often pursue ventures that defy short-term profit logic. What sustains them is not a spreadsheet, but a story—a narrative that links their actions to their values.

Purpose provides that narrative. It serves as a decision-making filter, clarifying trade-offs and reducing cognitive overload. In an age of infinite options, this clarity is essential. The phenomenon of decision fatigue, well-documented in psychology, erodes willpower and impairs judgment. But when purpose is clearly defined, many decisions become obvious. A founder who knows their company exists to democratise education does not waste time chasing luxury brand partnerships. A business rooted in environmental ethics does not compromise on supply chain transparency. In this way, purpose is not a vague ideal—it is a time-saving heuristic.

Moreover, mission-driven leaders exhibit what researchers call "future self continuity"—the ability to connect present actions with long-term identity. This temporal coherence increases patience and reduces impulsivity. It encourages investment in systems, relationships, and capabilities that may not pay off immediately but are crucial for sustainable growth. In contrast, when goals are driven solely by extrinsic markers—revenue targets, prestige, market share—entrepreneurs are more likely to chase short-term wins at the expense of long-term health.

One striking example of these principles in action is the story of Warby Parker. Founded with the mission of providing affordable eyewear while addressing global vision care inequity, the company embedded purpose into every layer of its business model. Its founders—motivated by both commercial ambition and social conscience—created a hybrid model that donated a pair of glasses for every one sold. This clarity of mission not only differentiated the brand in a saturated market, but galvanised employee engagement, customer loyalty, and investor confidence. Their growth was not in spite of their purpose. It was *because* of it.

Contrast this with businesses that have lacked moral clarity or authenticity. The fall of WeWork, once a darling of the startup world, illustrates how a compelling narrative unmoored from coherent purpose can collapse. The company's vague slogans about "elevating the world's consciousness" masked a business model riddled with operational inconsistencies and governance issues. Despite initial capital inflows, the absence of real alignment between mission and mechanics proved catastrophic. Purpose, when performative, becomes a liability. When embodied, it becomes a multiplier.

Purpose also has contagious properties. Neurological research into mirror neurons and social cognition suggests that people subconsciously adopt the emotional states of those around them. Leaders who are visibly animated by mission inspire similar engagement in their teams. This emotional synchrony fosters trust, cohesion, and psychological safety—conditions that amplify innovation and reduce attrition. A leader's passion, when rooted in authentic purpose, becomes a cultural catalyst. It is sensed, not stated.

Furthermore, purpose-driven businesses often attract values-aligned customers and investors, which has measurable effects on cost of acquisition, retention, and capital efficiency. Customers increasingly buy not just what a brand sells, but what it *stands for.* This behavioural trend is especially pronounced among millennials and Gen Z, who consistently favour brands that reflect their ethical and environmental concerns. Behavioural economics teaches us that identity congruence—when a consumer's self-image aligns with a brand's message—increases purchasing likelihood and lifetime value. In this way, mission is not just a moral imperative; it is a market differentiator.

This synthesis of neuroscience, psychology, and behavioural economics reveals a compelling truth: purpose is not a peripheral concern for entrepreneurs—it is central to peak performance, sustainable strategy, and authentic leadership. It fuels the brain, grounds the emotions, sharpens the mind, and clarifies decisions. It is the invisible architecture beneath resilient businesses, the quiet force that turns commerce into contribution.

Yet purpose is not a static thing. It must be revisited, interrogated, and refined. Neuroscience reminds us that the brain is plastic—capable of change and growth throughout life. So too is our sense of mission. What begins as a personal conviction may evolve into a broader movement. What starts with one founder can ripple into a collective. The task is not to lock purpose in a vault, but to keep it dynamic—responsive to new data, feedback, and lived experience.

In the end, the real promise of purpose-driven entrepreneurship is not simply that it leads to financial success, but that it leads to *meaningful* financial success—wealth that is not measured solely by net worth, but by contribution, coherence, and integrity. The science tells us this path is not only possible. It is optimal. And for those willing to lead with both intellect and intention, it is the most powerful kind of success there is.

Features Candid Interviews with Impact-Driven Entrepreneurs Who've Successfully Built Profitable Businesses Without Losing Their Mission

In the age of growing scepticism towards capitalism's motives, the idea that a business can be both profitable and principled often meets with incredulity. Yet beneath the headlines of unicorn IPOs and hyper-scaling tech empires lies a quieter, more enduring movement—entrepreneurs who have built financially robust enterprises while remaining deeply tethered to their original purpose. Their stories are neither tidy nor formulaic. They are textured, candid, and often marked by difficult choices. But they offer one of the most compelling arguments for a reimagined economic ethos: that profitability and integrity are not mutually exclusive—they are mutually reinforcing.

One of the most resonant voices in this space is that of Sasha Dingle, founder of Mountain Mind Project. A former elite athlete turned mindfulness educator, Dingle built her organisation on the principle that mental health and performance are not opposites but allies. From its inception, her business model was infused with values drawn from trauma-informed care and contemplative science. When she was advised by consultants to "professionalise" the brand and shed its meditative roots for broader appeal, she resisted. Her reason was simple: her mission was not to scale a mental fitness app, but to deepen human awareness. Rather than diluting the vision to appease investors, she redesigned her offerings to attract aligned clients—people who valued presence as much as performance. Over time, her client base grew, not in spite of her principled stance, but because of it.

What makes Dingle's story notable is the deliberate decision to trade fast growth for fit. In a world conditioned to celebrate acceleration, that choice is radical. And yet, the data increasingly validates it. According to the Edelman Trust Barometer, consumers are four times more likely to buy from brands that they believe have a meaningful purpose. The trust premium is real, and for founders who stay true to their mission, it translates directly into loyalty, word-of-mouth referrals, and long-term sustainability.

Another case that illuminates the interplay between mission and margin is that of Kresse Wesling, co-founder of Elvis & Kresse. This British luxury brand began with a bold proposition: to rescue London's decommissioned fire hoses from landfill and turn them into high-end accessories. From the start, 50 percent of profits were pledged to related charitable causes, including the Fire Fighters Charity. Wesling and her partner faced pressure early on to abandon the profit-sharing model and retain earnings for reinvestment. But they saw their profit model not as a hindrance but as a statement of identity. The clarity of this commitment attracted discerning customers and collaborators, including a long-term partnership with Burberry to upcycle their leather offcuts. Today, the brand is not only financially successful, but an exemplar of circular economy principles in action.

Wesling's approach underscores an important insight: impact is most credible when it is operationalised, not ornamental. Many entrepreneurs today are tempted to posture as mission-driven while maintaining extractive or opaque internal systems. But those who embed purpose structurally—whether in ownership models, supply chain ethics, or reinvestment strategies—build businesses that are not only more respected, but more resilient. They do not weather crises by pivoting to virtue; they endure because virtue was baked in from the start.

Consider also the story of Jason Ballard, co-founder of ICON, a startup using 3D-printing technology to build affordable housing. Unlike many in the property-tech sector, Ballard's motivation was rooted not in disruption for its own sake, but in solving one of humanity's most urgent challenges: shelter insecurity. His team's mission was not simply to innovate, but to democratise access. When venture capitalists expressed concern that the company's social ambition might undermine profit potential, Ballard responded by sharpening both: designing pilot projects with NGOs in Mexico and Haiti to demonstrate both feasibility and humanity. The result was a wave of interest—not just from philanthropists but from governments, private investors, and global architects. ICON's valuation has since exceeded hundreds of millions, but its founding ethos remains intact. It's not simply a 3D-printing company. It's a housing equity company that happens to use frontier technology.

What these entrepreneurs share is a refusal to compromise on what behavioural economist Dan Ariely calls their "meaningful irrationality." They are not driven solely by market logic. They are motivated by internal coherence—a sense that their work must make sense not just financially, but ethically and existentially. And this irrationality, far from hindering them, often sets them apart in a market increasingly saturated with superficial differentiation.

Moreover, the interviews conducted for this book reveal a common pattern of risk-taking that is undergirded by mission, not ego. These founders were not reckless. They were *anchored.* Their clarity of purpose gave them the confidence to defy prevailing norms—to ignore scaling playbooks that didn't fit, to delay monetisation in favour of testing models that honoured their values, to say no to capital that would come at the cost of culture. They did not avoid risk. They chose the *right* risks—those that aligned with long-term impact over short-term metrics.

One of the most personal and moving stories came from Asha Mehta, a financial strategist who left a high-ranking role at a hedge fund to create Global Delta Capital. Her goal was to leverage financial systems to invest in underserved economies, particularly those led by women. At first, colleagues in traditional finance scoffed at the idea. But Mehta believed that integrating ESG principles and gender-lens investing wasn't a political statement—it was smart economics. She built a team rooted in both rigour and representation, and her firm has since outperformed many of its peers while remaining deeply focused on impact. Mehta's journey illustrates that purpose is not incompatible with complexity or scale. It can, in fact, serve as a strategic differentiator in systems that are overdue for reform.

These stories challenge one of the most persistent myths in entrepreneurship: that idealism is a liability. On the contrary, the candid interviews collected throughout this book suggest that mission is the most enduring form of capital. It outlasts trends, inoculates against burnout, and fosters a depth of customer and employee engagement that no advertising campaign can manufacture. But only when it is real. These entrepreneurs were not merely talking about change—they were operationalising it. They were willing to let their mission shape their models, even when it meant slower growth or steeper learning curves.

What makes their stories particularly instructive is not just the outcome, but the process. Each of them wrestled with doubt. Each of them faced temptation to dilute or delay their purpose. And yet, through discipline and reflection, they chose integration. They refused the binary between doing good and doing well. They pursued the *harder path*—but the one that made them proud to show up every day.

As readers reflect on these interviews, the takeaway is not to imitate the particulars of any one model, but to absorb the deeper lesson: that the future belongs to those who can hold paradox. To those who can be both strategic and soulful. Analytical and aspirational. Grounded and visionary. The entrepreneurs featured in this book are not perfect. But they are pioneers—proof that it is possible to build companies that honour both humanity and commerce. And in doing so, they have given us more than business models. They have given us a glimpse of what the next economy could look like—if we have the courage to build it.

Includes Interactive Elements Like Mission-Mapping Worksheets, a Burnout Barometer, and Decision-Making Frameworks to Ensure Readers Take Action

One of the persistent criticisms levelled at books on purpose, leadership, or entrepreneurship is that they often inspire without enabling. Readers finish the last chapter moved by the message but left unsure of what to actually *do* with it. The gap between insight and implementation becomes a chasm, and without structured guidance, even the most motivated individual risks retreating into the comfort of routine. To address this inertia, this book was deliberately designed to be more than a set of ideas. It is a practical system—anchored in evidence, refined by experience, and structured through interactive tools—that transforms abstract understanding into meaningful action.

Each interactive element embedded in these chapters serves a specific and strategic function. They are not decorative add-ons, nor are they academic exercises. They are intervention tools—mechanisms to disrupt automatic thinking, illuminate blind spots, and scaffold behavioural change. Among these, the Mission-Mapping Blueprint, Burnout Barometer, and Values-Based Decision-Making Framework stand out as core instruments that support entrepreneurs in aligning their vision with viable, sustainable action.

The Mission-Mapping Blueprint is perhaps the most foundational of these tools. It invites readers to move beyond vague notions of purpose and into the architecture of applied intention. Many entrepreneurs can articulate why they started their business in emotional or visionary terms, but struggle to express that mission in ways that influence pricing, hiring, product design, or strategic planning. The blueprint challenges users to reverse-engineer their business from the end state they desire—financial, emotional, and societal—and work backward through clear pillars: personal values, customer outcomes, operational levers, and sustainable revenue pathways.

This technique draws on cognitive behavioural psychology, particularly the principle of mental construal. When we imagine future states with specificity—naming not only the outcome but the pathway and the obstacles—we increase our likelihood of follow-through. The blueprint compels the entrepreneur to make these imagined states tangible. For instance, a founder who dreams of creating equitable education access must define what "equitable" means in practice, how it will be measured, what trade-offs it may require, and how it affects the unit economics of their model. By the time the exercise is complete, the founder has not only clarified their mission but operationalised it. They are no longer guided by aspiration alone—they are guided by a plan.

The Burnout Barometer, in contrast, is not about vision but preservation. It addresses the often-overlooked cost of being a purpose-driven entrepreneur: chronic overextension. Research from organisational psychology shows that individuals driven by moral conviction or a deep sense of impact are more vulnerable to emotional exhaustion. The same fuel that propels them—meaning—can also become a trap, leading them to justify unsustainable workloads, underprice their labour, or neglect recovery. The Burnout Barometer provides a diagnostic snapshot of this dynamic. Through a series of calibrated questions rooted in the Maslach Burnout Inventory and adapted for entrepreneurial contexts, it helps founders assess not only physical exhaustion but emotional depletion, cynicism, and a declining sense of efficacy.

Crucially, the tool doesn't stop at measurement. It includes interpretive guidance and structured interventions. For example, if a founder scores high on over-responsibility and low on resource regeneration, the tool suggests specific strategies—reallocating decision-making authority, redesigning feedback loops, or instituting protected non-working hours. This process is informed by behavioural science findings on self-regulation, showing that self-monitoring combined with micro-adjustments is one of the most effective ways to interrupt burnout before it becomes incapacitating. And by linking these insights directly to mission alignment, the tool reinforces a core thesis of this book: that sustainability is not peripheral to purpose—it is a prerequisite.

The third key instrument is the Values-Based Decision-Making Framework, which addresses a problem that plagues both solo founders and executive teams: decision fatigue. In a landscape saturated with options, entrepreneurs often find themselves paralysed or defaulting to expedient choices that subtly erode their original intent. The framework acts as a compass, enabling decision-makers to evaluate options not only through the lens of profitability or scalability, but also through fidelity to their values.

Drawing from decision theory and moral psychology, the framework prompts users to evaluate any given opportunity against five core filters: alignment with mission, long-term consequences, stakeholder impact, resource efficiency, and emotional congruence. This multidimensional approach helps prevent common decision-making biases, such as overemphasising short-term rewards or succumbing to sunk cost fallacies. It has proven particularly useful in situations where entrepreneurs are choosing between growth opportunities—say, between accepting funding from an investor with questionable values versus bootstrapping to maintain autonomy. The framework does not prescribe the "right" answer. Instead, it surfaces the *right questions*, enabling reflective and intentional leadership.

These tools, when used in combination, create a virtuous cycle. The Mission-Mapping Blueprint sets the direction. The Burnout Barometer safeguards the leader's capacity to execute. The Decision-Making Framework ensures that choices made along the way do not dilute the mission but deepen its expression. Together, they form a self-regulating system—a kind of internal governance for mission-driven entrepreneurship.

Their effectiveness is borne out not only in academic research but in real-world application. Entrepreneurs who piloted these tools during the book's development phase reported increased clarity in strategic planning, reduced anxiety around growth decisions, and a heightened sense of personal alignment. One founder, leading a climate-tech startup, noted that using the Burnout Barometer forced him to confront how his personal overwork was undermining his team's morale. Another, a creative entrepreneur balancing freelance work with a social impact initiative, used the Decision-Making Framework to identify which clients were actually subsidising her purpose—and which were eroding it.

What unites these testimonials is a shift from reactive to reflective entrepreneurship. The tools do not offer easy answers. They demand rigour. But in return, they offer coherence—a state in which thought, action, and ambition align. This coherence, as behavioural economics suggests, is one of the strongest predictors of long-term perseverance and authentic success.

The inclusion of these interactive elements also signals a departure from the traditional model of authorship. This book is not designed to be passively consumed. It is a dialogue. A provocation. A working manuscript for your enterprise. And that is intentional. Because the truth is, purpose cannot be absorbed. It must be constructed. And construction requires tools.

By embedding these tools into the book itself, the reader is not only empowered to think differently—they are empowered to act differently. They are invited to become authors of their own frameworks, curators of their own energy, and architects of businesses that do not merely respond to the market but help reshape it.

In a world that often values speed over substance, scale over soul, these tools are an invitation to build differently. Not slower, but more deliberately. Not smaller, but more sustainably. Not perfectly, but with integrity. They represent the difference between knowing what matters and living what matters—and in that difference lies the future of meaningful, mission-driven success.

Offers a Science-Backed but Deeply Personal Perspective on Redefining Wealth Beyond Traditional Measures

For decades, the definition of wealth has been dominated by narrow metrics—net worth, annual income, portfolio diversification, and market share. These indicators, though undeniably important within conventional financial frameworks, have long failed to capture the complexity of human aspiration. In recent years, however, a growing convergence of research from neuroscience, psychology, and behavioural economics has begun to challenge the primacy of monetary accumulation as the sole marker of success. Instead, these disciplines are painting a more nuanced portrait of wealth—one that is not only richer in data, but richer in meaning.

At its core, this book advances a science-backed but deeply personal case: that wealth is not merely what you *have*, but how you *live*. It is not only about freedom from financial stress but about coherence between values, vocation, and vitality. This redefinition is not philosophical embellishment—it is rooted in robust evidence that ties well-being, purpose, and financial outcomes together in a dynamic system of reinforcement or erosion.

From the standpoint of neuroscience, researchers have found that the brain's reward system responds differently to purpose-driven outcomes than to purely extrinsic rewards. The mesolimbic dopamine pathway, often activated by financial gains or social recognition, also responds to altruistic acts and meaningful accomplishments. But crucially, the neurochemical signature is more enduring when the reward aligns with a person's internal values. In practical terms, this means that entrepreneurs who build businesses grounded in mission experience more sustained motivation and resilience than those chasing success defined by external validation alone.

This neurobiological insight is mirrored in psychological frameworks such as eudaimonic well-being—the Aristotelian concept of flourishing through purpose and virtue, now validated through decades of empirical research. Psychologist Carol Ryff's widely cited model identifies six dimensions of well-being: autonomy, environmental mastery, personal growth, positive relationships, purpose in life, and self-acceptance. Notably absent is financial capital. While money can support some of these dimensions—such as autonomy or environmental mastery—it does not guarantee them. In fact, studies consistently show that after basic needs are met, increases in income contribute marginally to life satisfaction, especially if the work generating that income is misaligned with personal values.

This divergence between income and well-being becomes even more salient when viewed through the lens of behavioural economics. Daniel Kahneman and Angus Deaton's landmark study in 2010 famously found that emotional well-being plateaus at around $75,000 USD in annual income. Beyond this point, additional earnings have diminishing returns unless they are tied to a sense of meaning, control, or contribution. More recent studies, such as those by Matthew Killingsworth, nuance this finding by showing that happiness can continue to rise with income—but only when people use money in ways that reflect their values and enhance their lived experience. In other words, *it's not what you earn, but what it enables.*

This shift from wealth as accumulation to wealth as alignment represents not just a theoretical evolution but a profound personal reckoning. When entrepreneurs begin to interrogate what success *feels* like—not just what it *looks* like—they often discover a misalignment between their metrics and their motivations. This book includes interviews with founders who, despite external appearances of success, experienced a hollowing-out—a sense of alienation from their own businesses, a fatigue that success could not cure. For them, the redefinition of wealth was not an intellectual exercise. It was a survival strategy.

Take the example of Anjali Mehta, a tech entrepreneur who sold her first company for a figure most would consider "life-changing." But within two years, she had spiralled into burnout, questioning the value of everything she had built. In her words, "I had money, but no meaning. I'd won the game—but I'd never stopped to ask if it was the right game to begin with." Her second venture was different. It was smaller, slower-growing, but centred on a social impact mission related to digital inclusion. Financially, she earned less. Psychologically, she was *wealthier* than she had ever been.

These stories are not outliers—they are warnings. They caution against the seduction of metrics divorced from meaning and advocate for a model of entrepreneurship where profit is not abandoned, but recontextualised. In this recontextualisation, new forms of capital come into view: emotional capital, relational capital, intellectual capital, even spiritual capital. These are not sentimental abstractions—they are real assets that affect business performance, resilience, and legacy.

To operationalise this broader definition of wealth, the book integrates interactive tools designed to provoke reflection and decision-making aligned with individual values. The Mission-Mapping Blueprint helps readers identify financial goals that support a life vision, not distract from it. The Burnout Barometer measures not just workload but energy alignment—a crucial but often overlooked determinant of long-term effectiveness. And the Values-Based Decision-Making Framework ensures that strategic choices remain tethered to purpose, especially under pressure.

Each tool draws on behavioural science principles such as implementation intentions, affective forecasting, and cognitive reappraisal. These are not incidental techniques. They are deliberate applications of research that show how reflection, when structured properly, increases the probability of sustained behavioural change. And behavioural change is what ultimately redefines wealth—not by erasing traditional financial goals, but by embedding them in a richer matrix of meaning and well-being.

Crucially, this redefinition is not prescriptive. It does not suggest that everyone should build a nonprofit, reduce their income, or prioritise mission over margin. Rather, it asks each reader to define what *enough* looks like on their own terms. For some, wealth may still include significant material abundance—but with clear boundaries on how that abundance is sourced and used. For others, it may involve downscaling, not as a retreat from ambition, but as a return to alignment. The only universal principle is this: true wealth is internally coherent. It feels like integrity, not imbalance.

This perspective is particularly important in a cultural moment where the narrative of constant growth is increasingly under scrutiny. Ecological economists and sustainability experts are beginning to echo what psychologists and philosophers have long understood: that infinite growth is neither possible nor desirable. In this context, redefining wealth is not only a personal act—it is a political one. It challenges the assumptions of a system that rewards accumulation without accountability, expansion without reflection.

The entrepreneurs featured in this book did not reject wealth. They redefined it. They refused to be reduced to metrics that failed to honour the full spectrum of their humanity. And in doing so, they built lives—and businesses—that are not just profitable, but *profoundly* satisfying.

That, ultimately, is the invitation this book extends. Not to abandon ambition, but to interrogate it. Not to demonise money, but to reimagine its purpose. Not to settle for success, but to seek significance. To define wealth not as a destination, but as a way of being—rooted in purpose, animated by values, and sustained by a vision of a life well-lived.

Because when wealth reflects who you are, not just what you earn, it becomes more than a number. It becomes a force. One capable of shaping businesses, communities, and futures worth building.

About the Author

Nico Farouq is a business strategist, conscious capitalism advocate, and speaker dedicated to helping entrepreneurs align profit with purpose. With a background in international business and social innovation, Nico has worked with startups, non-profits, and Fortune 500 companies to build ventures that thrive financially while staying true to their values. His writing combines deep business insight with an inspiring call to action for a more ethical, human-centred approach to money and enterprise. Mission-Driven Money reflects his belief that the most successful businesses of tomorrow are built on purpose today.

www.ingramcontent.com/pod-product-compliance
Lightning Source LLC
Chambersburg PA
CBHW031344230926
51848CB00002B/375
* 9 7 8 9 3 7 1 3 4 1 0 8 0 *